C000216617

Watch Over My Life

What Will Be - Book One

Laura Ashley Gallagher

First published in 2021

Copyright © 2021 Laura Ashley Gallagher

All rights reserved. No part of this publication may be reproduced, stored in a retrieval system, or transmitted, in any form, or by any means without the prior permission of the publisher.

Set in 12/14 pt Garamond MT Std

ISBN: 978-1-5272-9079-2

Visit www.lauraashleygallagher.com to read more about Laura Ashley and her upcoming releases. You can sign up for her e-newsletters so that you're always first to hear about her new releases, updates and exclusives.

DEDICATION

To all the amazing women,
no matter the colour of your ribbon,
head up, stay strong, and be proud to fight like a girl.

ACKNOWLEDGMENTS

Thank you,

To my parents, for the support, encouragement, and unconditional love.

To my sister, for sharing my tears and, most of all, the laughter.

To my husband, for always holding my hand and showing me the meaning of true love.

And to the most amazing son, thank you for teaching Mommy what pure, unconditional love is, and to never be afraid to be silly.

ONE

Do you ever get the feeling you've forgotten something?

Jessica Connors had that feeling from the second she walked out of his house this morning until just five minutes ago when she realized what she had forgotten was her underwear.

She sat at her desk, tangled her fingers in her dark auburn curls, and read the same line of the book five times before it dawned on her that she had already read it. She loved her job as a book editor; always gave one hundred percent, and goddamn it, this book had to be on his desk by tomorrow morning.

But today her mind was elsewhere. She couldn't get him out of her head—his big brown eyes, his short cut dark brown hair, his skin rubbing gently against hers. It replayed like a movie in her head. He touched her so lovingly and with so much care that she almost believed him. The thought of his kisses trailing down her body made her want to jump ecstatically from her seat and yell at the top of her lungs.

No!

She had to stop with these thoughts. They were ruining her. She never acted like this, and it was time for her to get on with her work.

But he was so damn unforgettable. He hadn't stopped floating around her head since she'd woken up this morning and saw his muscular body sprawled out against the bedsheets.

Then the guilt came along to crush her. The unbelievably heavy thumps pounding in her chest made her want to throw up, and her head ached with the pain.

The loud, echoing sound of the phone ringing knocked her out of her trance.

"Hello," she answered, her voice trembling.

"Good morning, Jessica. I have a call for you on line two," the young receptionist, named Sophie, sang through the phone.

Why did everyone sound so chirpy this morning? First, there was the teenage girl in the coffee shop—there to make some money for her weekly cinema trips with her fellow giggling teeny boppers. She just stood there patiently, like a robot, a never-ending pearly white smile beaming over the counter. And she was still grinning, in her own little world when numerous people continued to change their orders, asking for unbelievably detailed coffee. For the love of all that was holy, coffee was coffee. How hard could it be?

And now there was Sophie. The pretty redhead receptionist sounded as if she were on top of the world.

"Jessica?" Sophie's voice repeated, waiting for a more educated reply than silence.

She could feel her heart pound in double speed, making her pulse race and her palms sweat.

"Oh, yes, of course. Put them through."

She pressed the number, anxiously waiting to hear the voice she dreaded on the other line.

But did she really dread that voice?

No, and she hated she could admit it to herself.

She dreaded what the voice would say, what it could do to her senses. That voice could take over her entire body if it wanted to, just as it did last night. It could take her to new heights. But those heights were usually three feet off the floor, on a bed with silk sheets, and his hot, male flesh hovering above her.

Sweet lord above, get a grip on yourself.

"Hello?" a low hum came through the speaker of the phone. The husky voice sounded almost lost.

"Thank God," Jessica let out. That voice may have sounded lost, but she would have known it anywhere. It was her friend, Sharon. At any other time of the day, she might have tried to avoid their long conversations because she knew her friend would complain about something. But right now, she embraced the fact Sharon was calling. She even embraced her complaining like a warm, fuzzy teddy-bear.

"Is that you?" Sharon spoke.

"Yes, it's me," she confirmed, not fighting away the smile on her face from the sheer relief.

"What the hell are you doing? I tried to ring your mobile. Where is it?"

Jessica's eyes narrowed, confused. "It's in my bag. You know me, I probably have it on silent," she explained, lifting her black leather handbag from the floor next to her chair.

"Anyway," Sharon continued, "Melissa is having her baby shower tomorrow. You are coming, right?"

"Yes," Jessica answered, distracted as she rummaged through her bag, feeling her pulse quicken as each second ticked by and she couldn't find her phone.

"Good, because you are my victim. Grown people babbling about shit-stained, hungry, crying little humans, makes me want to vomit. Why the hell she went and got herself pregnant baffles me anyway," Sharon went on.

"Maybe because she just got married, and she wants to start a family," Jessica grunted, rolling her eyes. Her friend was never the best for understanding situations she was not involved in.

Again, Sharon baffled on in something rather incoherent to Jessica's ears.

"Shit."

"What?" Sharon questioned.

"My mobile, it's not in my bag. Shit. Shit. Shit."

She remembered seeing it on his bedside locker this morning. She left in such a rush, doing her best not to wake him, she must have left it behind.

"I left it on his locker." She slammed her palm on her wooden table, feeling like a complete idiot. Now she was going to have to face him again. Not that she could avoid him, but she was planning to keep a low profile for at least a week.

"Excuse me! Did you just say his locker?"

"Shit," Jessica repeated. She had just given herself away to her best friend. Now she would have to tell her something she had deeply intended on keeping a secret; a dark secret that would give her chills when she thought back on it and dreamed about it in the comfort of her mind.

But that's all she wanted it to be.

A memory.

Now she would have her best friend remind her every time she had too much to drink that she slept with the one man she hated.

"Come on. Spill," Sharon demanded, her voice rising in pitch from the excitement. That girl could smell gossip. "You can't just say something like that and expect me to let you get away with it."

Jessica huffed loudly, feeling defeated. "I slept with someone," she muttered quickly, trying to avoid mentioning his name.

"Jessica Connors had a one-night stand? You go, girl. Get yours."

"Ugh! I'm not proud of myself."

"Who was it?" Sharon sounded serious now.

Jessica bit down on her lip, deliberating if she should tell her the truth or lie and make somebody up.

Who was she trying to fool? Sharon could read her like a book, she always could, and Jessica had to face that she would never get away with not telling her; no matter how hard she tried.

"Well?" Sharon prompted.

"I can't believe I am saying this." She took a deep breath and swallowed the embarrassment boiling in her throat. "I slept with Jake," she said in a bare whisper, fearful that if too loud, she would have to admit it to herself.

The phone went silent.

She waited for a moment.

Then more silence.

And more silence.

"Shar-"

But she cut her off with the loudest scream she had ever heard in her life. She kept the phone at arm's length. Far enough to be sure her eardrum would not burst.

"You slept with Jake!"

"It's not funny," Jessica persisted through gritted teeth.

"I know. I think I'm laughing from shock. It's a nervous reaction." Her hysterical behaviour trailed off. "Okay, wait a minute. I can't believe you slept with Jake," she said seriously. "Let me recap for a moment, just to make sure we are talking about the same person."

As if she didn't know.

"Is this the absolutely gorgeous, Jake Williams, who can, and does, have any woman he wants? The Jake who you do and always have despised? The same Jake you almost fainted over because you walked into work one day and found out he was your boss?" Jessica felt sick to the pit of her stomach.

"He is not my boss," she demanded.

"He is a partner in the company. He's your boss. Get over it. So, it's that Jake, huh?"

"Obviously, what other Jake is there?" Jessica shouted, annoyed at the continuous questions and the reminder of everything Jake was to her. As if it had slipped her mind by some miracle.

"Hey calm down. Don't get your knickers in a bunch. Is that what happened last night? He got your knickers all bunched up, and you had to rip them off?" Sharon teased.

"You are not helping."

"Sorry." But her tone didn't match the meaning of the word. "So, how did all of this happen?"

"Look, can we talk about this later? I have some work to do."

"Eventually, you have got to come to terms with it. Avoidance will eat at your soul, but for now, I will leave you off the hook because, believe it or not, I have work to do myself."

Jessica doubted it was actual work. She was probably feeding on a poor newbie who wanted to further his career, and Sharon had given him false promises. Jessica swore she was a vampire, thirsting for the blood of those she could take advantage of. She wasn't being mean about it. Sharon did it plenty of times before, and she wasn't ashamed to admit it either. If it was for her gain, it was fine.

"I will call around later for all the gossip. I will bring ice-cream."

"Good. I will need it."

But, of course, because Jessica had the worst luck in the world, it wasn't long before the phone buzzed to life again.

"Another call waiting on line two."

Jessica sighed heavily, feeling annoyed. Sharon always did this; rang back the second time because she thought of a joke she could tease her with.

"Sharon, I told you I will see you later. I have work to do," she breathed, rubbing the tips of her fingers over her temples.

"You weren't thinking about work last night."

Jessica thought her heart had stopped. Her pulse quickened, and she could feel the beads of sweat forming on her skin.

"You okay down there?" he asked, waiting for her to answer. "No. Actually, you were great down there. Sorry, wrong use of words on my part." And the confidence that boomed through his laugh made her want to vomit. Even so—that single vibration of his voice box also made her want to rip his clothes off.

Vomit or rip his clothes off, make up your mind!

"You're sick, Jake," she spat.

"Be in my office in twenty minutes. I have two things belonging to you." She could hear the sex dripping in his tone, and it scared her because it was his voice and his way with words that made her succumb to him the night before.

"I have your phone and something…" he hesitated for a moment, "rather lacy."

Then the line went dead.

Sweet divine. Her heart was about to explode from her chest with anxiousness. What the hell was he talking about? Her mouth went dry; suddenly realizing.

Whoops! He had her underwear.

TWO

Jessica found herself having to stop as she reached the floor of his office. She needed to compose herself. She couldn't let him see her like this.

Sharon was right, and she needed to face it. He was her boss, and there was nothing she could do about it. Well, apart from never looking at the man sexually again. She could keep her distance, couldn't she?

Then why on earth was she reacting this way?

She could hear the blood pound furiously behind her ears. Her pulse was beating so fast it made her breath sound like tiny explosions as it escaped through her slightly parted lips, and her tongue felt like sandpaper against the roof of her mouth. Her slim shoulders tensed, and she shivered fiercely as a cold sweat crept down her neck. She couldn't let him see her like this. She had to come across as if last night was nothing more to her than some casual sex. A moment of weakness.

She had to let him think that, at least.

Convincing herself was a different story.

She knew it was wrong, but she never felt so compelled to someone in her life. Honestly, it scared her when she couldn't resist him because who on Earth has sex with a man they hate?

Reminding herself to curse her idiotic and abnormal behaviour every few minutes wasn't difficult, considering she couldn't get him out of her mind.

But in reality, when she asked herself, and if she was truly being honest, did she regret it as much as she should have?

She felt the guilt. Nothing else could describe the knot in her stomach, burning as a constant reminder of how stupid she was last night. She should've been stronger and stood her ground, but she didn't even have a ground to stand on. As corny as it sounded, when he touched her the way he did, she felt she was floating ten feet in the air. His kisses, her fingers tangled in his hair, the sheer pleasure of him, the way she shivered with his very touch.

She bit down on her glossed lip to suffocate the heat radiating throughout her body.

Damn heat.

But at this stage, she needed a whole river to extinguish the flame burning right to her very core.

She passed the ladies' bathroom, stopped, and retraced her steps. She needed to splash water on her face and relieve her skin of the furious blush spreading across her cheeks.

Luck was on her side—the bathroom was empty. Jessica turned on the cold tap and let it run for a moment. Then she cupped her hands under the cold water and raised them to her face. She let the cool sting slap some sense into her.

"Get a grip on yourself, girl. You are better than him," she muttered under her breath. "You are worrying over nothing. It's Jake, for Christ's sake. It's the same man that used to joke around with you when you were six for being chubby." She grunted loudly, once again grateful the bathroom was empty.

She never forgot it. Jake was two years older than her and grew up with Jessica's older brother. He used to tease her constantly for the extra puppy fat she carried around, but he stopped when she confronted him one day and gave him an unmerciful kick into the one sensitive area of his manhood.

She acted tough, but Jake didn't know how he made her go home at night and cry because she had a serious crush on him.

She got over her crush and he got over the name-calling, but when Jake asked her out on a date, her childhood crush was once again her everything. She was smitten and dressed up in her best blue dress. Her mother even styled her curls.

He stood her up for Shelly Murphy. The school slut, with a liking for a constant cold butt; her skirts rode up far enough.

That wasn't fair. Jessica was just jealous of her long legs.

But Jake broke her heart that day, and he never even acknowledged it.

She was never one for holding grudges, but Jake was lucky. She made an exception for him.

And it wasn't just that. Maybe it was his ways, his all too charming ways with every woman who crossed his path. It sickened her when she met him at a club and had to watch as ten different women drooled over him. It made her want to stick her fingers back her throat in disgust. But what made it even worse was that he indulged in every second.

Shaking the irritating thoughts from her head, she took three deep breaths, breathing in some confidence. She brushed down her black pencil skirt and tucked her white shirt inside. Bunching her loose curls together in her hand, they bounced over her shoulders and down her back in loose wavy spirals, and for a moment she let her eyes close.

All her five senses were taken over by him with just a single thought. She could still smell his scent like she could when he stood close to her; she could feel him just the same as when his body trapped hers between his arms; she could taste him on her tongue, see him in her mind, and hear the infectious words he whispered to her.

Her mind spiralled back to a single moment when he was looking down at her. Instinctively, like an animal, she raised her bare thigh, sliding it along his waist. It didn't take long for him to grab it, pulling her even closer; his breath trembling as he brought his hot lips to hers. Then, as he trailed his kisses over her collarbone, he ran his tongue along her neck and quickly blew cool air over the moisture his lips had left.

It took everything for her not to leave out a moan right there in the middle of the ladies' restroom.

Stop doing this, a voice in the back of her head warned.

"Right, it's now or never," she told herself before heading in the direction of the door and into the hallway.

Jessica's stilettos pounded on the tiles as she walked down the lengthy hallway towards his office.

Her heels had never pounded before. Everything was amplified, including her heart. Her fingers twitched nervously by her side.

"Good morning, Jessica." Those were the voices of people busy at work to her right.

Her mouth was too dry to speak, so she just smiled and waved, suppressing the urge to scream, "No, it's not a good morning, it's horrible." But those people didn't do anything to her. It wasn't their fault she ended up naked this morning.

She wanted to cry.

His door was open. The light filtered through into the corridor as she approached his office.

Usually, her reason for coming here was to pick up a book, not her underwear.

She was so stupid sometimes. How did she forget her underwear? They kept her area warm. If her mother knew, she would get a lecture on how not wearing underwear gave her pneumonia.

But she straightened up, looking more confident than she felt.

She turned to see him; his broad shoulders, the way his lips turned up into a soft, amiable smile, and his muscular body looked like a god in a black button-down shirt. And God forgive her, she had to hold back a growl.

He seemed to be in deep conversation with somebody on the phone, speaking loudly about a business meeting he attended a week previously.

She was deliberating whether to walk away. She had a legitimate excuse if he asked her why she never came to see him. She wouldn't want to disturb a phone call. It might be important.

But she couldn't face coming back. She mustered the courage once, and each second she stood there, frozen, her courage melted away. She needed to 'grow a pair of balls,' as her brother would say.

Or larger ovaries.

Concentrate Jessica, you're stalling. There was the voice again.

Jessica tapped twice on the glass of his office door, his head immediately jerking up.

"Sorry, I have to go, John. There is someone extremely important here to see me. I'll call you later."

She couldn't help but feel the heat under her cheeks as he stared at her, eyeing her up and down with that ridiculous grin on his face.

"I could have come back," she told him.

"Don't be stupid. Come in." He gestured to the leather seat. "Close the door," he added as she walked into the office, feeling her heels sink into the smooth, black carpet.

That's new, she noted.

Dragging her legs to his desk seemed like a mile. She thought her knees had turned to water. She needed to sit down before she collapsed right there in front of him.

Feeling the blood rush through her like acid, she took a seat in the chair opposite him. She glanced around quickly, avoiding his heated stare as she waited for him to say something.

But he said nothing. Instead, he gazed at her so intensely she had to look away again in fear she might get lost in his eyes.

"Will you stop staring at me?" she barked, shifting in her seat. It made her uncomfortable when he looked at her like that.

His lips curved up into a half-smile. "You're too sexy for your own good, Jess."

She just rolled her eyes, turning her head away from him to look out of the large window and up into the cloudless powder blue sky.

Last year, Jake became a partner with the Lynwood Agency. Jessica was working there for two years when one day, she was introduced to her new boss.

She was almost hospitalized for shock, and Jake was almost hospitalized for severe brain damage.

She wanted to kill him. And not just in a figure of speech way. She wanted to injure him; slowly.

"My phone. Do you have it?" She finally gave in and said something. The silence was crushing her.

"Straight to the point, like always." He smirked, and she felt glued to the chair. "Come on, Jessica, we have lots of time and a very big table. And your phone is all the way over here."

Her head tilted to the side, her eyes widening, and her lips parted, breathing cold, sharp air.

Was he serious? Did he want to have fingers left to play around with his lady friends? If he didn't give her the phone, she was going to break his hand.

She looked straight at him for a long moment, and she knew by the look in his eyes, he was serious.

This guy is an even bigger asshole than I thought.

But sitting there, staring at him, Jessica thought it more appropriate to punish him in another way. If that was the way he wanted to play, she was in the game. Why not indulge him a little?

She wet her lips, sliding her tongue over them before biting down on the skin. She looked at him in the most seductive way she knew, allowing heavy breaths to sweep away the light strands of hair from her face.

Immediately, he straightened and stiffened in his chair.

"You're right," she agreed, her voice smoky and almost a whisper. "It's a big table. We could do so much on this table. Don't you think?"

He just nodded like a robot, his eyes wide.

"And I do need my phone. And it is all the way over there." She pointed while picking up her hair, letting it fall to one side, down her neck, and over her shoulder. She played with her silver necklace while rubbing her fingers along her collarbone.

She watched him swallow hard in anticipation.

He was wondering what she was going to do next. Maybe slip under the table? She assumed he enjoyed viewing the sight of women on their knees.

She knew she was his prey, and he was just sitting there, enjoying the view and building the energy to pounce.

She leaned forward, resting her elbows on the wooden table, allowing him a cheeky peek at her cleavage.

Standing, she let out a shaky breath as her fingers traced the grains of wood, and she began to walk towards him.

"Things could get very interesting on this table." She moistened her lips with her tongue.

"Definitely." He gave her that stupid smirk again, pushing his chair out slightly as she stood in front of him.

Pressing her palms against the table, she propped herself on top of it, and rested her legs on the arm of his chair. She leaned forward, moving closer to him so she could whisper in his ear. Involuntarily, her breathing became heavier the closer she got. Feeling his cool breath sweep across her neck, once again the goosebumps prickling her body threatened to shatter her to pieces if he came any closer.

She had forgotten what she was going to say to him.

Then he stood, fitting perfectly between her legs. The heat from his body swept against hers. And if he didn't stop, his idea of office fun on the table would no longer be a joke.

"The thing is," she began, trying to keep her cool while running her finger down the black material covering his toned torso. How she wanted to just rip the material away and uncover the beauty of what was beneath. She could feel his breathing become more frantic against her skin and it took every ounce of courage not to just tell him to take her; that she was completely his. "This place has rules, and it's against the rules to sleep with your boss." She couldn't help the soft cry when he pressed his wet lips to her neck.

"Come on, Jess. I have known you way too long to be just your boss." His voice strained with an urge.

She closed her eyes, letting the chills take over her body as he ran his fingers up her arm and down her back.

"Jake." She gasped as those same fingers glided over the bare flesh of her thigh. With a firm grip, he held it high against his waist. She hadn't even noticed him heightening her skirt.

"Me and you," he blew a breathless whisper against her ear, "We don't need rules."

She took a deep breath then and tried not to concentrate on how close she was to being naked. She gently slid her tongue along his neck, but just once, before pressing her lips to his ear.

"Well, sorry," she murmured, finally feeling some courage filter through. In a way, she wished she didn't have the courage, but it was for the best. "I like the rules. Now give me the goddamn phone," she hissed, sitting up to face him, pushing his hand away from her thigh.

Reluctantly, he handed her the phone, disappointment written all over his face.

"Christ, you are hot," he groaned, eyeing her up and down, another hot blush creeping onto her cheeks. "Oh, wait..."

She tried to remove herself from the table. Or maybe it was more like peeling herself from the table. Her legs were still wrapped around his waist. He opened the drawer to reveal some black lacy panties.

He raised his brows, swinging the material around his fingers before he said, "Aren't you forgetting something?"

Jessica sat back slightly, scrutinizing him, a smile playing on her full lips.

"Sweetheart," she began, "those aren't mine."

He blanched.

"But.... but.... Yes, they are," he stuttered. "You were wearing these last night?" It was half a statement, half a question. "Yes, you were. I remember them," he said, fully convinced.

"Jake, I'm disappointed." She tutted. "I can't believe you brought me some other girls' underwear. I have standards."

He looked lost and utterly confused.

"But... But," he stammered once again. "Jess, I'm so..."

"Gotcha," she teased, nudging him playfully. "They're mine. Don't look so worried." She almost cackled, grabbing them from his hand and placing them in her bag. "Now, get out of my way. No hanky panky from me today."

She pushed him back, granting her space to stand. Pulling her bag onto her shoulder, she fixed her skirt in her best attempts to maintain any dignity she may have left. Jake sat back in his chair, still looking at her with a mystified expression. Probably confused about what he was going to do with the sudden stiffness in his pants.

"That was cruel," he spoke as she turned around. "But unbelievably sexy."

"Two can play that game, Jake." She winked, tilting her head to the side.

"Yeah, yeah, now get that fine ass of yours out of my office before I carry you to this table."

"And by the way."

"Yes, gorgeous?"

"I will have the book on your table first thing tomorrow morning," Jessica confirmed professionally, turning to leave.

After all, their relationship was strictly business. Anything beyond that was not acceptable.

THREE

"Ice-cream," Sharon squealed, waving two tubs of vanilla ice-cream in the air as Jessica greeted her at the door.

"Good. Come in." Jessica sighed, giving her friend a lazy smile, and feeling even more depressed than she was when they first spoke. Now, on top of last night, she had this morning playing games on her mind. She was tempted to give in to him; let his body control her until she couldn't take it anymore. And some part of her regretted she didn't.

It seemed everywhere she looked, there was sex. She was walking down the street and a group of girls were talking about it. Every billboard was drenched in the forbidden lust that was swarming around her. Sex, sex, and more sex. That was all she could hear, and frankly, she was getting sick of it.

She stood there, wrapped up warmly in her sweatpants and a large jumper. Even the curves of her body were completely lost in the bulky sweater.

Her apartment wasn't huge, but it was perfect for what she needed.

Her sister was an interior designer. She helped to pick out the latest trends and colour schemes for the apartment. They decided on warm colours for the living area. Rich cream walls with a chocolate brown sofa; the gold and brown cushions thrown loosely onto it. Her curtains were gold, draped over the large window, which gave her the wonderful view of the city lights. A large rug covered the space on the wooden floor in front of the television.

"You look depressed. As in eating lots of chocolates depressed. That's not good. Sit. I will get the spoons." Sharon rushed, already removing her coat as Jessica snuggled up on the large sofa. She knew her friend wanted to hear all the gossip as soon as possible.

"So, how the hell did this mess happen? I mean, it's Jake," Sharon reminded her, handing Jessica the ice-cream, removing her shoes, and practically jumping on the sofa.

"Hate is a very strong word," Jessica suggested, surprised at how uncomfortable she felt when Sharon said it.

"You know as well as I do, you have never gotten on with that man. It's like you two repel each other. You both walk in opposite directions if you see one another getting too close. Don't get me wrong, I always said you two are suited. You are hot, and he is so ridiculously hot. It's a lot of hotness right there in one couple."

"Are you coming onto me?" Jessica joked, taking a spoon of the ice-cream before letting it melt down her throat.

"I'm just stating the obvious." Sharon shrugged, licking her spoon. "Now stop changing the subject. How did all of this happen?"

"I had a book due in for yesterday, but when I went to give it to him at his office, he wasn't there. His secretary strolled into my office with her six-inch heels stomping all over my lovely wooden floor. She handed me a note. It wasn't anything unusual. He often sends me notes to tell me things or when he is too busy to come and see me personally."

"I'm sure he comes to see you personally all the time," Sharon interrupted, giggling like a schoolchild.

"Seriously, do you want to hear this story or not?"

"Sorry." She pouted, raising her hands in surrender. "But one last question. Why does he need the books when you're finished with them?"

"Only if it's one of our big clients. He's head of the publishing department, and he's a little obsessive. Although, why he's head of publishing, I don't know. It's not where his background is."

Jake's background was in media. The Lynwood Agency also has a media department, and she swore when he became partner, he chose publishing just to torment her.

"We know why," Sharon scoffed, confirming Jessica's suspicions. "But that's for another day. Back to the note."

Jessica went on. "It said to drop by his place later that night to give him the book and sorry he couldn't be there to take it from me earlier. That wasn't anything out of the ordinary. I've been to his house many times. Surprising as it may seem, we work well together."

"Uh-huh," Sharon agreed, edging for more.

"When I went by, he invited me in. I couldn't say no. It was pouring outside. I went in and gave him the book. We talked about a few things at work and then... Then, he just.... He just...," she stuttered. This part still confused her. She just didn't get it.

"Spit it out!"

"He just kissed me," she whispered, rubbing her fingers over her mouth, feeling the sensation of his lips moving with hers.

"You mean, just like that? He just kissed you?"

"Yes," she said softly, mesmerized by the scene replaying in her head. "It wasn't exactly what I was expecting."

"That is so sweet," Sharon cooed over her ice-cream. "It's romantic. Then what happened?"

She rolled her eyes. "I think we both know what came next."

"You went from kissing to being naked on his bed? I like your style, Connors." Jessica couldn't help but laugh a little. "Sleeping with the boss like that. I never knew you even had it in you. Not only did you sleep with the boss, but you slept with Jake. I know, the same person, but it's Jake." Her laughter eased off and her face relaxed into a more somber expression. "I think he likes you," she finally said, smiling gently while taking another mouth full of ice-cream.

"He doesn't like me, Sharon. He used me for the sex and that was it."

"So how was it?" she asked eagerly. Her eyes widened in anticipation.

"I will not answer that."

"Is love/hate sex the best? You know, they say it is? Bet you christened the entire house with your hotness?"

"Sharon! You are not all there upstairs, are you?" Jessica complained.

"No, but how is he downstairs?" Sharon erupted into a fit of giggles. "I'm your best friend. I'm supposed to know these things. Was he good?" she pressed as a cruel smirk infected her lips.

Jessica felt the blood rush to her cheeks and her face flushed with heat.

"Oh. My. God. He was!" Sharon screamed, almost jumping from

her seat. "I can't believe it. No wait, I can. Jake Williams. Sex God."

"Please stop," Jessica begged, lowering her head.

"Was I right about the whole house thing, too? Bet you made use of the shower, huh?" Sharon persisted. "I saw the shower when he first moved in. Water comes at you from all angles."

"You are disgusting."

"I'm right, though, aren't I?" Sharon smiled smugly.

Jessica closed her eyes, trying her best to hide her embarrassment and to stop the truth from shining through.

"You are a filthy bitch." Sharon threw a pillow at her, hitting her arm with a thud. "Easily known you're a Scorpio. Your sex drive lasts forever." Sharon relaxed then. "I can't believe it. This is too much information for me to take in. I just can't handle it. You had sex with Jake," Sharon repeated, as if she were trying to let it sink in. "You have no idea how jealous I am right now."

"Yeah, right," Jessica grunted. "Pull the other one."

"I'm sorry, but have you seen the man? Well, obviously you have seen him. You've seen a lot of him. Those big brown eyes, those lips." She was lost in a daydream. "What I wouldn't do to that body. Not that I will have a chance now. I'm sure you showed him every trick in the book."

"What do you think I am? You make me sound like I sleep around a lot," Jessica droned.

"Sorry, sweetie, I know you don't. But it's the quiet ones you must watch out for," Sharon teased, poking her friend playfully. "So, what now?"

"We go on as normal."

"Normal? Do you honestly expect things to go back to normal? Jessica, you had the best sex of your life with your boss. Sweetheart, none of it even sounds normal. You are living in a fantasy world."

"No, I'm not. We can work together as we always have."

"Let me ask you two questions because we both know how I got my job, which I am extremely thankful for. What I am also thankful for is that my old boss is dead," she said coldly.

"Sharon!" Jessica gasped.

"Sorry, but it's the truth. Now, let me ask you two questions. Number one: was there anything about today remotely normal to you?"

That was an obvious answer.

"And number two: what have you been thinking about all day long and even now as I sit here with you?"

Jessica huffed loudly in defeat. Her friend was right, and she hated to admit it, but nothing about work today was normal. Lord above, she almost had sex with Jake on the office table.

Not normal.

And she was thinking about him all day long without a single break. Anytime she tried to concentrate or think of something else, his face or images of last night jumped around in her mind.

"See. I told you I was right."

Jessica bit down on her lip, feeling the blood pulsing under the skin. "What have I done?" she grumbled, sinking into the chair.

"If you want my advice, why not keep it going and get the most of him? Show him exactly what you've got. But honestly, I don't think he is going to let you go, Jess. I know he likes you. I've never seen a man look at a woman the way he looks at you. You walk into the room and it's like you are the only person he sees. But you're too damn stubborn to see it, and too scared to let someone in. But that's you, I guess."

"I don't think you could be more wrong about him liking me. But I'll figure something out," she assured. She hoped she would soon because she was afraid she would end up on an office table somewhere. It didn't even have to be a table. The floor would have been more than enough.

She threw her head back, frustrated.

This was going to be a hell of a week.

FOUR

That night, she tossed and turned until she was dizzy. The covers were too hot. The air outside was too cold. And everything was simply wrong. Every time her eyelids gave way to the tiredness, she would wake again, dreaming about random scenarios she couldn't remember.

She leaned her heavy head towards her clock. It was 6:30 am.

Time to get up, she decided.

For once, she could have a head start on the day.

She pulled back the curtains to a thin sheet of frost covering the window. The sunlight breaking through the clouds reflected on it like tiny crystals, and shone in rays of light throughout her bedroom, dancing in a proud outburst of colours on the walls. She opened the window a little, letting the bitter morning air caress over her skin. It stung, but it woke her with a violent shiver as goosebumps played along her flesh.

Stumbling towards the bathroom, she rubbed the sleep from her eyes, and turned on the shower to the hottest temperature she could handle. Slowly, she made her way under the sprays, letting the hot water relax and soothe her aching and tired muscles.

How was she supposed to face today and get through to the end? She was hoping to avoid him; maybe duck her head or sneak into the nearest bathroom when he came her way. But it was going to be difficult. She needed to drop off the book she was working.

But she had a plan. She was just going to walk in, leave it on his desk, and walk back out. Simple. She could do it. She *had* to do it. She couldn't leave herself as vulnerable as she did yesterday. And she was starting to believe Sharon when she said nothing was going to be the same. There was no other choice. She needed to make this right, and she'd be damned if she let other people find out what they both did. She was respected in her job, and she fully intended to have it remain that way.

Drying her hair, she allowed the natural curl to settle at the ends and dressed quickly in grey suit pants and a white shirt. After gulping down a cup of coffee, she grabbed her bag and stuffed her keys and the book inside it.

The drive to work didn't take long. She'd left earlier than usual, so the traffic wasn't as heavy. It was quite calm for a change. And that, for once, was a bad thing. She needed distractions. A mother shouting at her children on the school run. A young girl failing to apply her makeup at a traffic light. Anything to keep her occupied. But not today. Today, she got quiet streets and her agonizing thoughts.

Fantastic.

She parked her car in the nearest possible space, gathered her things, and headed towards the entrance. Deciding to take the elevator instead of fifteen flights of stairs, which, at that moment, were not looking all too appealing, she stood there and waited for the doors to open, amusing herself by silently counting down the floor numbers displayed above the elevator.

Finally, the enormous steel doors opened for her to step inside. She leaned her back against the wall, rested her tired eyes, and listened to the ridiculous music playing quietly in the background. But just as the doors were about to shut, a hand stopped them violently and her worst nightmare stood to look at her; a smug grin placed upon his face.

"I knew it was you. I would know you from behind any day."

She noticed him wink from the corner of her eye, but she refused to meet his gaze.

"Come on. Lighten up. I'm joking."

At that moment, she thought a need to glare at him with so much intensity, that if looks could kill, he should have been sprawled across the floor.

"I don't find it funny, so not today," she said, gritting her teeth in her best attempts to hold back the anger ready to boil over. "Can we just work as normal, please? Forget about the other night?"

"If that's what you want."

"It is."

"Fine," he agreed.

But his agreement was a lie, of course. This was Jake Williams. What did she expect? He wouldn't give up that easily. He never did.

He leaned forward, pressing his thumb against the red button. Jessica's heart skipped a few beats before it began racing in her chest.

Isn't that the button to stop the elevator?

The metal box came to a sudden halt, making her jolt a little, but her feet remained planted firmly on the ground.

"Christ, Jake, what are you playing at?" she shouted, but it felt like something trapped her voice, suffocating it in her throat from feeling her heart race deep in her chest. She tried to move around him in her best attempt to press the bloody button and make the elevator move again, but he blocked her. He didn't care that he was making her legs feel like jelly, or that her heart was beating so loud she could have sworn it was resonating all around them.

In her mind, she cursed herself because she had a sudden, animalistic urge to wet her lips with her moist tongue.

Keep that stupid tongue inside your mouth.

He scanned her face until his eyes landed on her lips.

Bad idea. Bad idea, she screamed in her head, her palms instinctively grabbing the metal bar behind her for support. Her pulse felt like bullets now, and her breathing? She didn't think she had any. It scared her to breathe around this man.

But she wanted that man so much, and he had put her exactly where she didn't want to be. She wanted to say something, but her voice was stuck in her throat somewhere and she couldn't find it.

"You're beautiful," he whispered in that painfully sexy voice of his, and in one sudden movement, he crushed her with his kiss.

She couldn't stop him, and the worst part was, she didn't want to. He cupped her face with his hands and pushed her back, pinning and lifting her against the elevator wall. His tongue grazed her full bottom lip, begging for entrance.

She let him! She really was insane.

His tongue slipped inside, exploring her mouth. Then his kisses travelled from her mouth to her neck and back along her jawline. Her breathing became more frantic.

Yes, she finally learned to breathe.

This wasn't right. She hated this man, didn't she? Why was she even questioning it? Of course, she hated him. Here she was, pinned against an elevator wall by the same man she lost sleep over the night before. The same man she ranted about so many times.

Jessica wondered how many other women he had pinned against this elevator wall before because he appeared to be an expert at it.

With that thought, and refusing to be a number to him, she found the strength to move her hands to his chest, and as much as it killed her to do it, she pushed him away. When he gently set her back on her feet, her chest was rising and falling madly, and it took every ounce of power she had not to pull him back.

"We have to stop this, Jake," she uttered quietly, out of breath from the excitement and the pleasures of having him touch her. For a minute, she felt alive again, but she couldn't allow this relationship, or whatever it was, to go any further.

"We do," he agreed, his eyes searching hers. "Sorry, a moment of weakness." His voice was crisp as he pressed that dangerous red button.

The elevator began moving again, but it felt like forever to Jessica before it stopped at the 15th floor. She took three deep breaths, trying her best to calm her pulse until finally, the elevator stopped, and the doors opened slowly.

"I have the book with me if you want it now?" she offered, holding the door.

"No. Bring it to my office."

Her face flushed of its entire colour.

"Don't worry, Jess. There won't be any funny business," he promised with one of his breath-taking smiles. She simply nodded and walked away, trying to catch her breath.

"Good morning, Jessica." Sophie smiled as she walked past. "Are you feeling okay? You look a little flushed."

Jessica's cheeks burned with embarrassment. "Yes, I'm fine. I'm warm," she explained.

Warm from being wrapped around Jake's body like a damn spider-monkey.

Quickly, she went to her office, leaving a confused Sophie behind.

It was all too risky. It needed to stop. She could not and would not let that happen again. It was too dangerous for them both.

She jumped, feeling her phone buzz in her bag. It wasn't until she went searching, she realized she was trembling. It was a text message from Sharon.

Sharon: You can do it. Resist the temptation.

Jessica: Awful timing. You could have texted me ten minutes ago. It would have warned me not to get in the damn elevator.

Sharon's reply was almost instant.

Sharon: Excuse me? What did you do in the elevator? And I thought you were the quiet one.

Jessica: Nothing happened. I promise. It's what almost happened. Anyway, I need to go. I will tell you later. Duty calls.

She slipped her phone back into her bag and sighed with discomfort when she saw the book staring her in the face. It only meant one thing: she would have to bring it to him.

It took her two hours to work up the courage to go. What happened in the elevator complicated her plan of just walking in and out.

She stood, the blood in her legs feeling like water, and grabbed the book before walking swiftly out of her office.

She looked confident, as always, but she didn't feel it. Not one bit. As each step brought her closer to him and that goddamn office table, she felt her heart beat insanely fast.

But there was something she hated even more than her heart doing gymnastics. It was butterflies. She felt like a teenager. Those stupid butterflies in her stomach fluttered around, making her breath catch in her throat. She'd trample all over those butterflies if she could.

Forcing a smile, she turned into his office but made a sudden halt. A man was sitting in the chair on the other side of Jake's desk. A man she recognized. His blond, sandy hair was cut short, and his blue eyes were prominent against his tanned skin. She would recognize those eyes anywhere. It was like looking in a mirror. A wide smile gripped her face.

"Oh my God, Pete. What are you doing here?"

He stood quickly, hearing her voice, and the urge was too strong not to run into his arms.

"Hey, little sis," he said, kissing her forehead. "I came in to see both of you. Don't worry, I was going to see you first, but I met Jake on the way up and we got talking. I was about to leave." He looked guilty.

"You're a horrible liar," she teased, slapping his arm. "I thought you were in Spain?"

Her brother travelled a lot. He taught English to students from all over the world.

"I was. The kids are on holidays, so I said I would make a surprise visit home to see everyone."

"Well, it's good to have you back. I missed you."

He pulled out a chair before sitting again.

"Sit. I haven't seen you in months."

"I have to get back to work. Call by my office when you finish here, okay?"

"Sure."

"Jake, I have the book ready for you." Her smile didn't seem so forced this time. Her brother was here, and she really missed him. But knowing her brother could read her just as easily as the book she was holding made her nervous. She tried to look normal—like she didn't sleep with Jake, and his tongue wasn't back her throat a few hours ago.

She placed the book on his desk.

"Thanks, Jess." He winked like he always did. He was the better liar.

"Maybe you can help me, sis," Pete said.

"With what?" she questioned, looking confused.

"See, we were sitting here, Jake and I." He chuckled. Why did he sound so weird? "And he had the biggest grin on his face. I know he's screwing someone. He just won't tell me who. Have you any idea?"

She almost choked. Her eyes became wide, and her face got hot. She looked at Jake, who appeared composed, but his eyes reflected her terror.

She shook her head. "How the hell would I know?" Her reply came out a little sharper than intended.

"You do work with him. There must be someone you know about?"

Was this all a joke? Had Jake told him what they did?

Never.

They might have been best friends, but she was still Pete's little sister, and Jake knew what it meant. Pete wouldn't have thought twice about jumping across the table to him.

"Who Jake has sex with is none of my business. He could have sex with everyone in this building; I really couldn't give a shit," she stated, keeping her cool.

That was a lot of *sex* and *Jake* in the same sentence.

Was winter always this warm?

And was that a pang of jealousy she just felt?

"Calm down, sis. It's not like it's you."

They both gulped, and she heard Jake swallow his nerves.

"I see you two haven't gotten over your differences, then?"

She rolled her eyes. "It's me and Jake. Will we ever get over our differences?" she deadpanned, knowing her brother already knew the answer.

"Whoever she is, she must be one hell of a sex buddy, because when I bumped into him, he was smiling so much it looked painful. You can't mistake the bounce in his step. Hope that girl knows what she is getting herself into."

"It's okay, Pete. This one is feisty. She can handle herself. I don't think I will bother her much, even if I try." Jake laughed, moving his gaze from Pete to Jessica and back again.

She was living in hell. Out of all the things that could go wrong, this was it. It was like some sick scene from a stupid comedy.

"Come on. Tell us who she is? I must know her if you're not telling me," Pete persisted.

Mother of pearl. Would he just give up?

"Believe me, you don't know her."

"Give me a name at least," Pete almost begged.

"Believe it or not, her name is Jessica."

Her mouth dried out like the desert.

"I didn't catch her second name."

"Typical," Pete huffed through his laugh. "I don't know her then because the only Jessica I know is you, little sis."

She smiled nervously in response.

"I'll be back in a sec. Nature calls," he said, leaving the room.

When she knew he was far enough not to hear, she turned and glared at the troublemaker, sitting comfortably behind his desk.

"What was that about?" she stuttered, frustrated.

"Don't worry, Jess. He doesn't know."

He was too confident. Too cocky. And he was getting on her last nerve.

"My brother is a smart guy, Jake. He can put two and two together and get four," she snapped.

She was pacing now. Jessica never paced unless someone had ticked her off. And it was extremely hard to tick her off.

Then he started laughing. A loud, booming laugh and her eyes travelled to his hard chest. Christ, this man was driving her crazy in every way possible.

Did he find this funny?

His voice echoed against icy walls and pushed its way into her ears, crashing down on her tolerance. Her hand tingled with the urge to slap him.

"Calm down, okay? He suspects nothing. As far as he knows, you hate my guts."

"I do hate your guts," she spat, shaking her head. "Tell Pete I had to go and to call by my office when he's done," she told him before storming out of the room.

That man did weird things to her emotions. One minute she wanted him, another she hated him.

It was times like this she needed a cigarette. She hadn't smoked since she was eighteen, and this is what he was doing to her.

Air.

She needed fresh air. It wasn't nicotine, but it would relax her trembling hands.

When she got back to her office, her brother was waiting for her, being nosy and rummaging through her stuff. But despite that, she suddenly felt calmer.

The rest of the day passed quickly, but it was mainly because she spent most of it talking to Pete.

That night when she went to bed, her eyes felt heavy with tiredness, but again she couldn't sleep. She tried her best to keep her eyes shut and breathe evenly.

Confused, she glanced towards her bedside locker, watching her phone flash, lighting up the room. She picked it up.

Jake.

Why was he doing this to her?

"Hello?"

"Hey, gorgeous."

She heard the deep voice and recognized it immediately.

"Jake? Is that you?" she questioned, playing dumb.

He sighed. He wasn't buying it.

"What do you want?" she asked, faking a sleepy voice, but she wanted him to think she was sleeping, and he had just woken her.

Because she shouldn't be losing sleep over this pain in her ass.

"See, I was at home, and you popped into my head. And I thought we were both at home alone when we could do different and better things together."

She chose not to take offense to him assuming she was alone.

He wasn't wrong.

She stood and strolled lazily to the living room. The cool air swept across her bare legs and arms.

"We both know the other night was great, and I know you want it to happen again as much as I do."

"Cocky much?" She grunted and heard his breathy laugh on the other end.

"I was thinking we should make use of our time."

She could just imagine the grin on his face.

"Jake, I'm not having phone sex with you."

"Who said anything about phone sex? Besides, who would want that when you could have the real thing?"

"What are you talking about?" she questioned, sounding worried, yet she couldn't help the excitement shining through her voice.

"Open the door, and I'll show you."

She almost dropped the phone.

"What?"

"Open the door," he repeated casually.

After standing as still as a statue with shock for a long moment, she finally made her way towards the front door. Slowly, she turned the handle, the phone vibrating with nerves in her hand.

And there he was. Looking like a god in his sweats and t-shirt. She could still make out his perfectly toned body through the loose shirt, and it made her want him more than ever. Jessica watched as his eyes scanned her from head to toe, and his tender lips curved up into a soft smile.

"Hello beautiful," he whispered.

Like earlier that day in the elevator, he didn't wait for an answer. Instead, he walked towards her and kissed her passionately. Just this time, it was softer. He closed the door with his leg as she wrapped her arms around his neck, bringing his body closer to hers so they could both feel the heat radiating from one another. The phone made a loud thud as it hit the floor, falling helplessly from her limp hand.

"You can't just turn up at my apartment like this." She was breathless as she pulled away from him.

"I know. But I did. So, goddamn it, I am going to kiss you," he said, wrapping her in his arms.

His tongue began exploring her mouth. Her body ached for him, and she wasn't about to let him go again. She didn't have the power. Not this time.

He lifted her, pinning her against the wall so her legs were firmly around his waist. He trailed endless kisses down her neck and then finally back to her mouth, his body flush against hers. She shivered as his hands, cold from being outside, gripped her thighs.

Every touch felt new to her. It was the excitement he gave her; it put her on a new high, and she couldn't resist him; no matter how hard she tried.

Still securely in his arms, he walked to the bedroom, where he placed her gently on the bed, crawling over her needy body to stare down at her.

And she was exactly where she promised herself she wouldn't be. But she loved the thrill. Besides, she was a woman. It would be sinful not to give in to those needs.

This is nature, she told herself.

And there they were, finishing exactly what they started in the elevator.

FIVE

As Jessica quietly closed the door behind her, she felt a sudden pang of guilt for leaving again. But she had to. She needed to be at work for nine and Jake… Well, Jake did what he wanted. After all, he was the boss. He could stroll in and out any time he liked.

When she woke, she watched him for a few minutes. Her body was still wrapped in his, as if he were protecting her in some sort of cocoon. She stared at his muscular chest, moving up and down with each even intake of breath. He looked consequently peaceful as his closed lids delicately hid his brown eyes; the same eyes she got lost in so many times.

She hated the thoughts of getting out of bed. She wanted to stay there, covered up with his warmth, but she was lying to herself by thinking he wanted the same thing. She wasn't that naïve. She knew exactly why he was there. But it worked for her, too. The last thing she wanted in her life right now was a man. She didn't have the strength to deal with it. She didn't need the complications of a relationship. There was too much at risk. She didn't want her heart to get broken, and she didn't want to drag someone else into her situation. Making someone's life complicated because of her 'issues' was not her goal. It wasn't fair to anybody.

Many times, she was told to live her life as normal as possible, and right now, that's exactly what she was doing. And she got herself a hot guy to do it with. Life was good.

She hoped he wouldn't take offence when he woke to the note she left on her pillow.

There is food in the cupboards.
Eat and get your ass out of my apartment.
See you at work.
Jess.

She dreaded seeing him. She knew all the emotions from the night before would come swirling back. Though she told herself countless times, she would stay away from him, and she could resist the temptation, seeing him standing at her door last night, daring her to give in. Her guard crumbled to pieces, and there was no hope of putting it back together. Even now, the thought of him made her want to run back to the apartment and wake him up with her uncontrollable kisses.

She no longer recognized herself. She didn't like letting her guard down and showing her true emotions. She hid them so deeply, sometimes not even she felt them. And letting other people see how truly vulnerable she felt was the scariest thing she could think of. Especially now. She didn't need anyone else to get hurt. It was better if she kept everything to herself. That way, she protected the people she loved the most.

She dwelt on it all the way to her office, where she threw her bag on the floor, sighing heavily when a pile of new paperwork appeared on her desk. Today was Friday, and she was looking forward to the weekend. She wanted to relax and be normal. She also wanted to go out and get heavily drunk.

Bad idea, she told herself.

She didn't know where she'd end up. Probably Jake's bed.

Yes, that was a bad idea.

The paperwork seemed to go on forever, but she finally finished it, signing her signature at the end, slipping it into a large brown envelope before handing it to Sophie to post.

She also had a new book to edit. She was looking forward to reading this one. It was untitled by a young, up-and-coming author. Her name was Elizabeth Harold; an enthusiastic, goofy girl who knew exactly what she was writing about and where she wanted to go with it. Jessica met with her once before and found her highly interesting. She could've talked to her for hours. When she found out Jessica was a book editor, she started sending some of her work.

She leaned back in her chair and took the thick book in her hands. She read six lines when she heard a light cough at the door. Her head popped up to see Jake standing there, his body leaning against the door frame with two coffee cups weighing in each hand.

He hates coffee, she thought to herself.

"Coffee?" he confirmed, offering her the cup as he held it up and strolled to her desk.

Unfortunately for her, she was dying for a cup of coffee, and thankfully for him, she was going to accept it.

"Thanks," she whispered, taking the hot cup in her hands.

He placed himself in the leather chair on the other side of her desk.

"People will talk, Jake. It isn't difficult to notice you walking in here with that undeniable bounce in your step." She smirked. "It's very gossip-worthy.."

"Let them talk."

"You know as well as I do, they need little to start a story around here."

"It's coffee, Jess. I thought you might need it. I know you have a lot on lately," he said, lifting the cover of the cup and blowing on the fiery liquid. She sipped on it slowly, letting the warmth slide down her throat.

"Worried about me, are we?"

"I'm your boss, and I know when you have a lot on."

The mention of him being her boss brought her straight back to square one.

"What are you doing here, Jake? My table is too small for any funny business and I'm seriously not in the mood." She was a poor liar, and he knew it. His smirk told her he didn't believe a word of it.

"You have a terrible impression of me." He grinned, and she couldn't help but smile back at him. "You left this morning?" It was more of a question than a statement of fact.

"I had to. I had to be at work by nine," she explained, inhaling the smell of coffee.

"I don't think I would've fired you for being late."

"I know, but as you said, I have a lot on. Someone has to work around here," she taunted, meeting his gaze.

He merely shrugged, staring out into the city. "What are you doing tonight?" he queried, looking back at her.

"I don't know yet, but it's not you," she replied, knowing exactly what he meant. He chuckled to himself, his laugh making his nose wrinkle. "I'm relaxing tonight and that doesn't include having sex with you."

"Do I tire you, Jess?"

"As a matter of fact, you do. Walking is a need I have."

"Thank you very much." He nodded, obviously pleased with himself.

She bit down on the inside of her jaw to stop herself from giggling aloud when he yawned.

"Do I tire you, Jake?" she repeated his words, leaning her elbows on the desk.

He looked at her and chuckled loudly. "I bought the coffee for a reason, Jess. I never drink this crap, but it keeps me awake."

Her cheeks heated with embarrassment. She made random notes on a page to hide it.

"Don't you have work to do? You could do better things with your time besides bother me."

"You're gorgeous, but that hurt," he teased, dramatically holding his hand over his chest.

"Get out!" she droned, throwing a pen at him. "Go on. Get out of my office. I have work that needs doing."

"Fine." He threw his hand up in surrender.

"See you at the meeting later." He winked before he left the room.

She hated those meetings. It was an hour of nothing. It was a meeting of twenty executive workers talking about how the company was going and certain issues they may have. She knew Jake hated it too. She often kicked him under the table to stop him from nodding off before it was his turn to address everyone. He pretended to listen to his two business partners, but he never did. Jessica knew the face when he tuned out of something and was in a complete daydream. He always looked too focused when he was in his own world. His eyes squinted, making it seem like he was doing math in his head.

Her phone buzzed to life on the table, bringing her back from her reverie.

"Hey, baby sis," she answered happily.

"Hello," her sister, April, replied sceptically. "Why are you so cheery? Who have you been screwing?"

"Am I only happy when I am screwing someone? I can be happy."

"I suppose," April answered slowly. "Hmm. Anyway, I'm calling to tell you that you need to come over tonight. Mom is cooking dinner for everyone because Pete is home."

"Great. What time?"

"About seven. And tell Jake to bring the fancy wine he always has."

Jessica blinked a couple of times.

"Please don't tell me Jake is coming tonight?" Her tongue stuck to the roof of her mouth.

"Jake is coming tonight," April stated dryly. "Get over it, Jess. Besides, you know the way Mom is with Jake. He's like a brother to Pete and me." April exhaled loudly. "Look, I really don't care why you two are so bitter towards each other. Just tell him not to forget the wine."

"Fine. I'll tell him," Jessica huffed, feeling defeated. "I have to go, April," she said before they both said their goodbyes, and Jessica rushed off to that hellhole of a meeting she needed to get to.

Thirty minutes later, there he was, doing it again. He was sitting next to her in the conference room with his eyes squinting, his nose wrinkling, and his mouth set in a hard line. He looked hysterical. But she promised herself she wouldn't laugh. Not again. She wasn't the only one staring at him, but for the other women, it wasn't about the look on his face, it was for his face, full stop.

Jessica tried to tune out as Mr. Johnson, another partner in the company, rambled on about how they could do more to save energy in the building. She despised these meetings. She never saw the point of her being there.

Scribbling in her notebook from boredom, she looked back at Jake, who still had that stupid look on his face. She wondered what he was thinking about.

Was he thinking about her?

Of course, he wasn't. Why would he? They may have slept together, but that meant nothing to him. He slept with women all the time. He never thought of them. So why would she be any different?

She wasn't. That was the point.

But it didn't stop her from wanting to be her mischievous self.

She bit down on her lip to hide the smirk tugging at her mouth. Her hand twitched with the want to touch him. And for once, she gave in to what her body wanted. She placed her hand under the table, ever so slowly and gently placing her fingers on his thigh and squeezing tightly.

Jake jumped. "Whoa."

"Are you okay, Jake?" Mr. Johnson asked, looking slightly concerned as Jake tried to compose himself.

"Yes. Yes. I'm fine," he explained, swallowing hard as she trailed her fingers up and down his thigh, smiling innocently.

"Okay." Mr. Johnson nodded slowly, looking unsure as he went back to rambling on about energy saving. Or at least that's what she thought he was talking about. She wasn't paying attention.

She pinched on her lip playfully with her teeth as she watched him stiffen in his seat, his body rigid as her hand grew closer and closer to the area she knew he was dreading yet longed for her to touch.

"Jess." He leaned closer to her ear, and she knew it was killing him to quiet the moan playing on his parted lips. His breathing was becoming heavier with every dance of her fingers. Higher and higher.

She suppressed the giggle bubbling in her throat and continued to look straight ahead at Mr. Johnson.

"Jess, we're in a meeting," he breathed, stuttering over his words.

"I know." She turned to look at him, her famous sparkle glinting in her eyes. "Revenge is a bitch," she whispered, moistening her full lips with her tongue.

As she continued, she finally reached the one area she knew would send him over the top. Her fingers massaged him softly, her palm playing along his suit pants. She watched him in amusement as he moved around in his seat, his hand rubbing over the beads of sweat on his forehead.

"That's it for today. I will see you all Monday," Mr. Johnson announced.

She didn't stop when people began packing away their belongings. She wanted to see him sweat a bit more. She slowly pressed against him, unassumingly pressing her lips to his ear. To anyone else, they were sharing a private conversation, but to Jake, he just received Jessica's moist tongue along his neck to behind his ear.

"Sweet Jesus," he let out and God forgive her, but she burst out with laughter. This was brilliant entertainment. "I'm sorry everyone," he apologized to his colleagues leaving the room, who had now turned around to see what all the commotion was about. "This damn table is really low down for my knees."

With a sexual act involved, he was a miserable liar. But all of this didn't stop his quiet moan sending thrills through her as she removed her hand. He looked disappointed as she stood. Positioning herself, she leaned over his shoulder, whispering in his ear, "The sweet joys of revenge. I don't think you should stand for a while. It might be obvious what we were up to under the table, and I don't think you would want everyone to know you are having sex with one of your employees." Her voice was serious.

"Everything okay down there, Miss Connors?" Mr. Johnson asked, narrowing his gaze. She straightened up and smiled.

"Everything is fine. I was just making sure Jake was okay. He was looking pale. But everything seems to be looking *up* now." She smiled, biting down on her lip to stop herself from laughing at the private digs she was sending to Jake while everyone else was oblivious.

"Okay, I will see you on Monday."

"See you later, Jake," Jessica simpered, parting her moistened lips.

The image of him sitting there in his chair, unable to stand with his mouth hanging open in shock, played over and over in her mind.

She felt evil, but with that man, she didn't mind.

SIX

"Hello, sweetheart." Jessica's mother, Rose, greeted her, swinging the front door open.

Her shoulder-length hair was straight, and her pale green eyes engraved with tiny wrinkles. Her petite figure had a red apron tied tightly around her curvy waistline, and her long, narrow nose wrinkled as she leaned over to kiss her daughter.

"Hey Mom," Jessica replied with a wide smile, kissing her warm cheek.

Jessica didn't need the homely and inviting smell to indicate her mother had been cooking. The heat from her skin and her blushed cheeks told her that.

"I feel like I haven't seen you in so long." Her mother frowned.

Jessica knew what was coming: a lecture about how she should call more. She only lived fifteen minutes away, but with all the work she had on lately, she didn't have the time to call around.

"You don't visit anymore." Her mother pointed at her. "And any time we see you, you are always rushing away."

"I have a lot on now, Mom. I promise to call more often." She smiled, repeating the words she said many times before while she made her way into the kitchen.

The smell of cooked food exploded through her senses, making her mouth water. Jessica always loved her mother's cooking.

"Well, you shouldn't work so hard. I think I need to speak with

Jake."

"I can handle myself."

"Did I hear my name mentioned?" a familiar voice interrupted, booming through the kitchen. Jake's powerful frame strolled in with a breath-taking smile spread across his face.

Rose may have wanted to have words with him moments ago, but Jessica could see his chocolate orbs were making her mother melt into a ball of mush.

"I brought wine." He winked, holding up two bottles of white wine before embracing Rose in a hug and giving her a soft peck on the cheek. "You are getting younger every time I see you," he complimented.

Her mother's cheeks flushed a pale red.

"You see more of me than my daughter does."

Rose took the wine and placed it in the fridge.

She's off again, Jessica thought.

"You'll tell me the truth, Jake. Is my girl working too hard?" Rose's brows furrowed in what Jessica didn't know was anger or sorrow.

"Mom, he doesn't keep a twenty-four-hour watch on me. I know when to stop. I'm fine," Jessica pressed, feeling frustrated.

"We both know how Jessica is, Rose. She loves her work, and she's pretty damn good at it, too."

"That's good. I suppose you always were a hard worker. I just worry about you. You always look so tired." Rose shook her head, taking a large bowl in her hand.

"Jeez, thanks. And I thought those night creams were working."

"I didn't mean it like that."

"I'm fine. Don't worry about me. You should worry about the hippie."

They all chuckled. She was talking about her sister, April. She always was unique. For April to feel herself, she needed to be different; different sometimes meant dying her hair an eccentric purple or piercing unnecessary body parts. Neither of which lasted long. Still, it didn't stop her from experimenting now and again.

"I thought she was going to run away with the circus. Remember the clown she used to date?"

Ah, Pedro. She dated Pedro for a month; also known as Tony the Clown. He was in town with the circus, and he fascinated April. Every night, Rose would stay up, waiting patiently for her daughter to walk through the door, pacing for every second she passed her curfew, in fear she had genuinely up and left with the circus.

She was merely seventeen, and Pedro was at least eight years her senior. An older man and the circus were both very tempting to April at that age, and Jessica was sure she contemplated more than once actually leaving with them.

"She gave me many sleepless nights, but someone has to love her," Rose joked, taking the bowl and pottering into the dining area, leaving Jake and Jessica alone.

"You look nice tonight, Jess," Jake mentioned, his voice sincere.

"Someone is full of compliments lately." She nudged against him playfully.

"It's the truth."

She placed her hand against his forehead. "Are you feeling alright?"

"Feeling fantastic. Unless you plan to play my nurse? In that case, I'm dying." He dipped his chin, letting his eyes droop.

"Shut up!"

"You're not totally off the hook. What was today about? People were asking if I was okay for twenty minutes."

The image of his helpless face flashed in front of her eyes, making her laugh.

"It's not funny," he demanded.

"I'm sorry, but it was hysterical. How I didn't laugh the entire way through that meeting is a miracle."

"You could have at least finished it."

"Oh, no. It wouldn't have felt so good to walk away then." Jessica winked, placing an evil look in her eyes.

"You're a tough woman."

"Jessica, will you bring me the salad?" her mother called from the dining room, interrupting their conversation.

"It's odd to see you out of your sexy business clothes," Jake said as she made her way to the countertop and tossed salad in a bowl. "I like this, though." He motioned his finger up and down, pointing to her body.

She blushed. She knew he was looking at the way her faded blue jeans hugged her bottom, and how her long cream jumper hung loosely from her shoulder, exposing her skin.

"Stop looking at my ass," she ordered, not even turning to look at him. Jessica knew him well enough to know where his eyes wandered to, and she couldn't help the heat from flowing deep within when she thought of it.

"I can't help it," he breathed, nodding his head.

"Oh, come on! Just help me with this stuff. We can't leave my mother to do everything."

"Being bossy suits you." He sniggered but gathered the serving bowls anyway.

"You two are so good. Jake, would you mind going to get everyone? They are in the living room."

"Not at all, gorgeous."

"Stop it now, Jake. I'll have to put you over my knee," Rose warned, suppressing the giggle.

"Don't threaten me with a good time."

Jessica stared at them, mystified by their behaviour.

"You two have such a strange relationship. If I didn't know any better, I'd think there's adultery being committed."

"You don't know any better," Jake goaded, kissing Rose on the cheek.

"Ah, don't be jealous just because he doesn't call you sweet names and say sweet things to you."

Jake and Jessica both looked at each other, mischievous grins threatening their lips; both thinking the same thing:

No, but you don't want to know the things he says to me, and they're far from sweet.

"I will get everyone," he said, disappearing out of the room before his eyes gave away their secret.

"He is such a nice boy," Rose expressed as they both set the table.

"He's thirty years old, Mom. He's hardly a boy."

"Yes, I know. Even so, he's always so charming. And look how far he has come, and yet he remains so humble. I'm proud of him. Such a talented young man," she murmured to herself.

Humble, my ass, she thought to herself.

But she couldn't deny his ambition, his work ethic, all while remaining grounded. He may have been a cocky asshole to her, but it's what they did. He knew it got on her last nerve and he played on it. She wasn't much better with him. And her mother was right. Jake was amazing at what he did, and he worked hard to get where he was.

"You two seem to get along a little better than you used to." Her mother glanced at her, knowing to thread this sensitive subject carefully.

"The night is young, mother, the night is young," Jessica sighed, not meeting her mother's eyes.

"There is my gorgeous little girl."

Jessica looked over her shoulder to see her father, Chris. Before she even had the time to say anything, he had her wrapped in a hug.

His black hair was now greying at the temples and had become lighter since Jessica's previous visit.

Has it really been that long?

She was the only one to inherit her father's big, ocean blue eyes and pale, porcelain skin.

"Everyone, take a seat. Dinner is ready," Rose ordered as she shuffled around the room. They all happily obeyed.

For a while, everyone stayed silent to enjoy the food with only a few words of small talk.

"So, Jake," Chris began, "Pete tells us there is a new lady in your life."

Why me? Why does it have to happen to me?

Didn't she already have her fair share of awkward moments for the day? She swallowed hard, trying to take away her unease, but it was no use. She could feel the beads of perspiration on her forehead.

"Oh, my God. Jake has a girlfriend?" April screeched in disbelief, at the same time flicking her long blonde hair behind her ears. "As in, you've had sex with her more than once?"

"April!" Rose warned sternly.

"Oh, come on, Mom. There's no room for Jake and girlfriend in one sentence."

Jessica and Jake glanced at each other as her heart pounded heavily in her chest, thumping so hard it pained her.

"What is she like?" Rose prompted, eager to hear more about the new love interest.

"It's nothing, really."

"Surely she must mean something."

Jessica watched him take three deep breaths. He wasn't prepared for this; she was sure of it.

"Well, she is very beautiful," he started, sounding serious enough for her stomach to do a somersault.

Jessica thought her heart had stopped.

"And funny. Bit of an evil streak in her, though. She knows how to surprise you when you least expect it." His eyes glanced around the table again, landing on her for a moment longer. "It's early days. I'm going with the flow, so who knows? And that should be enough information to keep you thinking. For now, I'm going to change the subject and get the wine." He stood nervously, patting his hands against his shirt, like the wine would magically appear from a pocket. Or maybe he was looking for his nerves, because she had certainly lost hers.

"I'm thrilled for you." Rose smiled as he walked away.

"Let's see how long this will last," April muttered under her breath before taking a mouth full of mashed potato. Jessica's hands tremble, her own fork shaking between her fingers. She dropped it before anyone noticed.

"I'll help," Jessica offered, raising her voice after him. She couldn't handle sitting there with her family talking about Jake's new sex buddy. It was too weird.

"That was awkward," she breathed.

He was already taking the wine from the fridge.

He nodded his head in disbelief. "You couldn't write it."

But she didn't reply, and he didn't have time to say anything else because the moment his eyes caught hers, she kissed him. She kissed him deeply, falling into the passion they shared with their lips.

She heard the bottle of wine clink down on the counter. Then his cold hands cupped her face, deepening the kiss with his tongue.

She had no idea what came over her, but it took control of her body. The sensation she received when he glanced at her took complete power over her.

"I'm sorry," she stammered, "I don't know…"

"Shut up, Jess." He quietened her with another kiss.

This time it was stronger, and she knew he wanted it too. She could tell by the way his hand gripped her hip and pulled her closer to him. His powerful arms lifted her onto the edge of the counter where, eagerly and aggressively, he roamed his fingers to her neck and skimmed down to her breast, tugging at her bra. She gasped and squirmed, tightening her hold around his neck.

"Jess," he quivered, vigorously kissing her tender lips, "I want you so bad, I'm afraid I'll take you right here with your parents in the next room."

She bit down and slowly opened her eyes. "And that wouldn't be a good idea," she added.

As they both silently pulled away, Jessica caught her breath. That was unexpected, but it felt amazing.

"You seriously know how to surprise a guy."

"Sorry, I didn't mean to just pounce on you."

"Stop apologizing. It was a kiss; a really passionate kiss, but don't be sorry for something that felt so right."

"Come on. We better get back in there before they get suspicious," she suggested, eager to get back to her seat and not look at his lips anymore.

"You're scared you'll do more than kiss me next time. Can't say I blame you." He shrugged, knowing the comment would get on her nerves.

"You're so full of crap," she groaned, stepping back into the dining room and taking her seat.

"Are you two at it again?" Rose gave out, waving her knife as she ate.

Jessica's cheeks turned hot. For a brief moment, she forgot they argued as well as had sex.

Relax, Jessica.

Jake entered the room moments later and smiled at her reassuringly. She was sure she was burning up.

Taking a sip of her wine, and then another, her mouth tingled as the tangy taste slid down her throat. She closed her eyes, fighting the familiar twisting in her stomach. The room was spinning, and her insides felt like they were heating. Somehow, though, she didn't think it was because of the wine.

Shaking it off, she tried her hardest to ignore it and involve herself in conversation, but it became increasingly impossible. The voices around the table became distant murmurs, and she swallowed hard to stop the nausea.

Not now, not here.

"Jess, are you okay?" Pete asked, his weary voice sounding from across the table.

"Am, yeah," she breathed, mustering up the power in her legs to stand. She tried her best to maintain her balance by gripping onto the edge of the table. "I'm going to use the bathroom."

It was a struggle to climb the stairs. The cold beads of sweat travelled over her collarbone and down her shirt. Tossing her body into the bathroom, she stood over the sink and let the cold water run for a few moments before cupping her hands underneath and splashing it on her face.

In the mirror, her eyes seemed paler than usual. There was a familiar tugging at her temples and the tingling in her face. Then the nausea started again until she could feel the bile rise in her throat. She leaned her head over the toilet to throw up the contents of whatever she had previously eaten. The pressure of the pounding pain in her head was increasing every second.

She hated how sudden this always was. Never a warning; it wasn't all that sympathetic.

Quickly, she washed her face again, flushed the toilet, and made her way back downstairs.

Seeing double wasn't her only problem now. Jake stood at the bottom of the stairs, waiting for her to land safely.

"I was coming to check on you. Are you okay?" His eyes narrowed on her, searching her face. The suggestive glint in his eye told her he knew something wasn't right.

"I'm okay." She half-smiled, trying to regain some composure.

She placed her foot on the last step, and her vision suddenly became blurred. The whole hallway spun. The cream walls seemed to merge with the table by the door. Then she felt her body sway to one side as her legs gave way beneath her.

"Fuck, Jess! You're not okay."

Jake's firm grip wrapped around her waist, and she shivered when the coldness of the wall met her back as he supported her body against it. She closed her eyes, needing everything to be clearer when she opened them.

Thankfully, it was.

His big brown orbs were seeping through hers.

"Christ, Jess!" She watched his chest rise and fall. "You're trying to give me a heart attack."

"Sorry," she whispered, unable to find her voice and out of breath. "Thanks for catching me," she said, standing straight. His hands were still on her hips.

"What's wrong with you?" he asked, his voice drenched with worry.

"It's one of my migraines," she lied.

"You're as pale as a ghost."

She swallowed hard, fighting away constant nausea. "Seriously, I'm fine."

"Jessica?" Her mother's voice echoed in her ears. "Oh my, are you alright?"

"I'm fine." She brushed away her mother's hands. She didn't need more people crowding around her. She felt smothered enough. "I think I should get going, though. I can feel a migraine coming on."

"Okay, honey. Go home, take something, and get plenty of sleep," Rose instructed, hugging her close for a moment.

The rest of her family soon followed to see what all the fuss was about. Just like before, Jessica assured them she was fine and told them she was going home.

The night air woke her a little, but her eyes still seemed heavy. Closing the car door, she leaned her head back when it opened again, and the violent shiver that crept down her spine from the bitter air didn't help the aching pain in her temples.

"Jake, what are you doing?" she snapped, looking up at him, sounding weak and feeling fragile. The dull streetlights reflected on his sallow skin and made his eyes glitter like crystals. His strong jawline flinched as he clenched his teeth together.

"You don't have a hope if you think I'm going to let you drive home. The only reason your parents let you out the door is because they didn't see what I did."

"You didn't tell them, did you?" She swallowed, feeling the beads of sweat running down her neck again.

"Of course not."

"Then, I'm fine," she persisted, teeth clenched and over the conversation already.

He crouched down outside the car, his eyes level with hers. His warm palm caressed her cheek, and the thrill from his touch echoed around her aching body, sweeping over her like a warm blanket. She leaned into his touch with a sigh, unable to stop herself. His fingers were in her hair, with his thumb brushing across her lips.

"Those beautiful eyes of yours are swirling in your head. Don't tell me you are fine."

"It's a migraine," she uttered, afraid to speak in fear the tears would stream from her glossy and blurry eyes. The pain was almost unbearable, but she couldn't let him see it. It scared her to be vulnerable around him.

"And it's dangerous to drive with a migraine. I'm bringing you home. We can pick up your car when you are feeling better. Come on. Get out and get into my car," he ordered, smiling weakly.

With a heavy sigh, she gave in, secretly appreciating his kindness. So much for not wanting to be vulnerable, but she didn't have the energy in her to argue with him. He was right, and for once, she had to get over herself and accept help.

Swinging her legs out of the car to stand, the heat of his hand was around her waist, helping her. She didn't protest because the street was spinning again, and she needed his support. Carefully, almost like she would break, he helped position her body into the front seat of his car and secured her with the belt. The smell of his new leather seats invaded her senses.

Cocky asshole.

She didn't hear him start the car, she only remembered it moving. Then her eyelids grew heavier and heavier until everything around her went black.

A slight tug at her feet awakened her. Reluctantly, she opened her eyes. She was in her bedroom. The curtains were closed, and the only light filtering through the room was the one from the hallway.

She jumped up, seeing a dark figure at the end of her bed. The pounding in her head was a reminder of why she was in bed to begin with.

"Hush, it's only me," Jake assured her.

"What are you doing?" she asked, out of breath from the fright.

"I'm taking off your shoes," he said, pulling the other boot. "Don't worry. I left your clothes on."

The hum of his deep chuckle danced around the room.

Her eyes remained on his as his strong frame walked to her side. He leaned over, kissing her softly on the forehead. His tenderness made her lower lip tremble.

"I'll be outside if you need me."

"Go home, Jake." He was far too big for her couch. "Don't stay here because of me. I'm fine, honestly."

"I'll go home when I'm convinced. Now, I'm only convinced you're a terrible liar."

"You can't sleep on the sofa. You can sleep here?"

"I don't mind sleeping out there. I don't want to make you feel awkward."

"It's not like we haven't slept together before. Besides, if you insist on staying, I don't want you sleeping on a cramped sofa. So, get your ass into bed. Just keep your hands to yourself," she warned.

"They'll be strapped to my side." He closed the door and removed his shoes. She pushed over slightly to make room for him.

"Come here," he said as he got in. He put his arm around her shoulder, and she snuggled into him, embracing the heat from his body. She was shivering uncontrollably, but it wasn't because she was cold. It was her body reminding her she wasn't well.

Pulling the covers over her shoulders, he whispered, "Wake me if you need anything."

"Hardly. I'm capable of taking care of myself," she told him, sounding firm and feeling an immediate pang of guilt. "But thank you."

"Stubborn," he muttered.

"I heard that."

"Good. You were supposed to."

After moments of silence, he kissed the top of her head.

"Goodnight, beautiful," he whispered.

"Goodnight, Jake."

Then the darkness of her sleep took over completely.

SEVEN

It was over a week since Jessica saw Jake. He went gallivanting on a fancy business trip that she made no-frills of refusing. Mr. Johnson had practically begged her to go. He called her his lucky charm. She guessed it was considering the previous two times she went, they secured the deal without a glitch.

But she wouldn't be used as a flirting tool for him to get what he wanted. Besides, she hated sitting there for two hours sharing dinner with people who knew absolutely nothing about reality and couldn't fathom a world existing where there were no limos, marble floors, and people to cater to their every need. She was getting tired of biting her tongue at those meetings, and she feared that soon, her teeth would miss her tongue and she would let loose on a rampage.

Nevertheless, they secured the deal without her this time, giving Jessica hope that Mr. Johnson would not ask her again.

Did she forget to mention that Jake brought his secretary? Watching that would make her gag. That blonde bimbo was going for more than talks on advertising. The only thing that girl knew how to advertise was herself. Seeing Jake's secretary swoon over him would have been as comfortable to digest as it would be to eat a crate of butter. The mere thought of her plastic breasts hanging on for dear life to stay inside her ridiculously low-cut shirt made Jessica's teeth grit viciously.

She sounded jealous, didn't she? Jealous wasn't her style. She was the girl that usually gave out about the jealous, obsessive freaks. Now she was turning into one. Wasn't that wonderful?

Her thoughts and nerves were frazzled.

"Tea or coffee, Miss?" a tiny voice interrupted her thoughts.

For a moment, she had to breathe in her surroundings.

The coffee shop. Right. That's where she was.

"Coffee, please," she answered, shaking the heaviness from her eyes.

She glanced across the table to where Sharon had her head buried in a menu.

"Hey, this may be your day off, but I only have an hour for lunch, so get your skates on."

"Relax."

Sharon then motioned the menu towards the young server, murmuring something to her as she did so.

"What's eating into your jolly-self today?"

"I didn't get much sleep last night. I'm a little tired."

"Did Jake call over again?" Sharon leaned her elbows on the table, edging closer; the intrigue plastered to her face.

"Jake? Ha! Don't make me laugh. I think he has fallen off the face of the earth. Besides, we haven't been doing anything like that," she lied.

She was angry, and she was even angrier that she was angry at him. She wasn't supposed to feel anything for him, not even anger. And the anger stemmed from missing him. She missed their nights together.

Get a grip on yourself.

"Why? What happened?"

This coffee shop didn't seem like the right place to explain to her friend the ins and outs of everything that happened, and frankly, she didn't think she had the courage.

"Come back to my office for a bit, and I'll tell you everything. For now, shut up and eat," Jessica teased, gesturing to the server carrying their lunch.

Almost an hour later and Jessica still felt like crap. Her head hurt from too many thoughts and her eyes stung from the tears that wouldn't fall. She needed sleep.

"Earth to Jessica." Sharon waved her hand in front of her face as the elevator doors opened, inviting them both with soothing music to step inside. "Are you alive in there?"

She glared at her friend from the corner of her eye.

"I'm good."

"Uh-huh," Sharon grunted, leaning back against the wall with an overdramatic hand movement.

Jessica knew that look. It was the look that made her whole face strain into something she could only describe as uncomfortable. Sharon ran her fingers through her bob-cut black hair and blinked over her grey eyes.

"What?" Jessica breathed, knowing Sharon was holding something back, and it was usually better to let her get it off her chest before she exploded.

"You're thinking about him, aren't you?"

"Excuse me?" Jessica turned her head, her eyes wide at the unwelcomed accusation.

"Don't play dumb with me. Jake. You are thinking about him. I can see it in those eyes of yours."

"I'm not thinking about him."

"Whatever you say. I wonder what Jake will say if he sees me going into the office?"

Jessica sighed.

"He won't give a damn. He probably won't be there. More than likely, he is too busy boasting about his new deal and convincing his new plaything to pump up the silicone in her boobs." Jessica rolled her eyes.

"Calm down, tiger! So that's what has climbed up your ass? Jake is banging Barbie?"

Jessica huffed outwardly and stayed silent. She was safer not saying anything.

As they stepped out of the elevator and onto her office floor, Jessica could feel the softness of the blue carpet she was walking on; her heels were sinking into it. She wished her entire body could melt into the floor beneath her.

She rounded the corner onto the long hallway where the modern, glass reception desk was located, with waiting chairs taking their place on the opposite side. The light blue painted walls made the place feel cold. Only the scattered flowers brought some warmth to the large space. But something else felt cold, and one look at the small huddle of laughing young women told her it was the smell of fresh, bitter gossip.

"He was incredible. I could have told you a couple of months ago," Jake's platinum blonde secretary boasted.

Her giggling made Jessica cringe—the way she would if nails glided against a chalkboard.

"I can't believe you had sex with the boss. What I wouldn't do to that man," Sophie went on, looking dazed.

"Everything okay here, ladies?" Jessica asked.

She never acted on it, but she was a senior figure in the business. She was their boss. She never played the boss card until they needed it. Right now, she felt annoyed and wanted to swipe the boss card right through them.

Still, her mouth went dry at the mention of his name. But it was the way she heard it and the words that followed that got her blood boiling. She knew she shouldn't have felt like this, but she did, and she couldn't help it. He didn't care about her, and she didn't know what possessed her to believe he ever did.

Immediately, they turned around to face her. "Good morning, Jessica." Sophie waved, a wide smile spreading across her pale-skinned face. Jessica didn't know the other girls by name, but she recognized their faces.

"Good morning, Sophie. Morning girls." She smiled and hoped it was polite. "This is my friend Sharon."

"Hi Sharon," they sang, like a clone of each another.

"Sorry, Jessica, we were just sharing the morning news," Sophie explained.

Jessica always shared a close bond with Sophie. She reminded her of her little sister, April—wild with a little innocence, and plain confused.

"What would that be?" Jessica questioned, sounding interested, shifting from one foot to another.

"Just that I'm the luckiest bitch in the world," the tall blonde almost screamed.

"Excuse me, but what's your name?" Sharon interrupted, and immediately the group straightened, huddling closer to each other, and obviously feeling intimidated by the stranger walking into their building. Hell, even Jessica felt intimidated, and she was with her.

"Ciara," she said, placing her freshly manicured hand on her slender hips.

"So, Ciara," Jessica continued, darting a glare at Sharon, "Why are you so lucky?"

"I'm just saying I had a lot of private time with Jake Williams for an entire weekend."

Jessica had to take three deep breaths as her pulse quickened in speed. For a split second, she admitted it was jealousy, but she quickly wiped the thought away. She wasn't supposed to be jealous. Jake was a free, good-looking man, who can do whatever he wanted with whoever he wanted.

"Are you sure you want to be spreading that around?" Sharon queried, mimicking Ciara's position by placing her hands firmly on her hips. The blonde blinked a few times, covering her green eyes, but finished with what sounded like a grunting noise.

"Wow. Someone is a lucky girl." Jessica nodded, not sounding the slightest bit enthusiastic. Nobody noticed though, apart from Sharon, who Jessica could tell was raging like a bull.

"I know. We're going for dinner on Saturday night. He just doesn't know it yet."

The entire group of girls giggled in unison. The only thing Jessica and Sharon had to do was merely glance at each other and they could read each other's thoughts.

"Oh, okay," Jessica dragged out, rubbing her finger over her lips. That girl hadn't a hope of getting him to go to dinner with her. Not because it was her, because he was Jake. He didn't date. Or he hadn't since Katie.

Jessica couldn't figure out what was tugging at her rib cage, but whatever it was, it hurt like hell, and she hated it.

"You can tell us, Jessica. You've known Jake for a long time, right? What is he really like?" Sophie asked, curious about the god-like man upstairs.

"You want my advice? Stay away. He is trouble, trouble and more trouble."

"It's a pity to hear you have that opinion of me, Ms. Connors." She heard the deep vibrations of his voice. He was so close she could feel his furious breath sweep across the nape of her neck.

Jessica didn't regret what she said, and he'd be damned if she was going to apologize. She couldn't hide the resentment in her eyes when she looked at him. It was too strong, too fresh, and she didn't have the energy, nor the courtesy, to be tolerant towards him.

"I think you girls should get back to work, don't you?" Jake advised the small huddle.

They soon scattered away, leaving the hall empty.

"Good to see you again, Sharon." He half smiled, barely turning to look at her.

"You too, Jake." She nodded.

Jessica turned to walk away, but before she could put one foot in front of the other, a firm grip caught her arm, sending shock waves through her with his mere touch.

"Can I speak to you for a minute?" He was staring at her like he could burn a hole with his eyes.

"I'm sure it can wait," she said, failing in her attempts to tug her arm away. He wouldn't let her go. She took a deep breath, giving in. They were going to have to sort this out sooner or later. She preferred sooner.

"You can head to the office. I will follow you."

As soon as Sharon disappeared, he began. "What the hell was that about?" he snapped. "You can't just disrespect me in front of the people that work for me."

"I wasn't trying to disrespect you as a boss, you know that. On a personal level, I thought I needed to warn that girl," Jessica defended herself.

"Against what?" His voice was becoming louder. His grip still wrapped around her arm, and the blood pulsed beneath her skin.

She couldn't tell him. She knew he was hardly touching her. It was the medication and the treatments. It made her more sensitive to pain.

"Against you," she spat, ignoring the throbbing in her arm. "You can't use her like that, Jake."

"I don't know what she said, but nothing happened. Nothing like that has happened since…" His features softened as he trailed off. But whatever he was thinking or going to say to explain himself quickly evaporated. His jaw stiffened, the same frosty glare slicing like a knife. "Are you jealous, Jessica?" he questioned, an icy, amused look on his face.

"Jealous? Are you serious?" She laughed, shaking her head. "Don't flatter yourself. I'm annoyed because you can't just use girls the way you do. And I don't mean me. I knew what you were like. I prepared myself for it, but I wasn't in it for anything else," she stated coldly. "Not like that poor girl, Carla or Ciara—whatever her name is. The girl thinks you love her. She may not have said it, but she thinks it. You have to stop using them. They are not pieces of meat or a toy made for your amusement." The anger boiled, and she bit down on her lip to stop it from trembling.

"Is this coming from the girl that wants to live every day like it's her last? What was it you used to say: 'Go with the flow, that sort of thing?' That's exactly what I'm doing." Jake threw her words right back at her.

The tugging at her chest began to build and build until the moisture stung her eyes.

"You are not living each day like it's your last. You are wasting them. And do you know what? Someday, you are going to wake up and realize you have nobody left."

She swallowed hard to soften the lump threatening to choke her.

"And you would know all about that, wouldn't you? Answer me one question. Who do you have in there?" He placed his hand over her chest where her heart was beating maddening beats against his palm. "Because you don't let anybody in."

Gradually, his voice was getting louder and the throbbing in her hand was beating stronger. Her blood was gushing, making the throbbing feel like gallons of blood struggling to fit through the tiny veins. As unwanted and hurtful memories swarmed around in her head, her mouth went dry.

The room. The screams. The fists.

A single tear trickled down her cheek. "Please, Jake," she whispered, pleading with him. Her heavy breathing was the only sound between them for a moment, her lungs desperate for more air. "Let go of my arm. You're hurting me."

He backed away quickly, watching her face with a pained expression. "Jess, I'm sorry," he apologized, wiping away her tears with his thumb.

"It wasn't you, Jake. It just reminded me…" she stuttered, unable to finish her sentence. His eyes widened in what seemed like both shock and fear. There was no hesitation when he pulled her close to him and hugged her tightly.

"Oh, baby, I never meant to do that," he breathed, kissing the top of her head.

She gave in, embracing him, and taking in everything about him until she could build up enough courage to let him go. It took all of ten seconds to do just that. He hurt her, and she hurt herself by letting him. She swallowed hard and backed away, feeling her heart sink into the lowest part of her stomach.

"So, here we are." She smiled, but it didn't reach her eyes. "Doing exactly what we always do. Fight. It's what we do. It's in our blood." She bit down on her lip. "Don't hurt that girl, Jake," she warned. She didn't want anyone to experience the pain she was feeling.

He was a robot, simply nodding, and she wondered why his anguished eyes were hurting her as much as it was hurting him.

Turning on her heels, she walked away, leaving him behind.

She found enough power to compose herself until she got into the bathroom. That was when she locked herself inside a cubicle, sunk to the floor, and sobbed away her wrenching pain.

EIGHT

"Jess?"

She wasn't sure how long she was sitting there on the cold tiled floor, letting the endless tears soak and dry into her skin. Her sobs had stopped, and her mind seemed empty. She couldn't think anymore; it took too much effort. Besides, the pain was enough company.

She mentally cursed herself for letting her guard down and falling into the same trap she had three years ago. A trap she promised herself she would do everything to avoid. She was suffocating, and a need to scream burned her lungs.

How had she let herself get this way?

She walked right into all of this with no protection. No armour. Nothing but a false exterior. She had nothing to steer her away from this pool of agony.

Jake wasn't like Rob. They were completely opposite, and as mad as she felt, she would never insult Jake by comparing the two men. But the trap was no different. Either way, one of them was always going to get hurt, and she couldn't do it. Not again.

"Jess, are you in here?"

Sharon!

She forgot about her. Quickly, she wiped her eyes and stood, feeling the blood rushing through her veins. How long was she sitting there? Her ass felt numb, so that should have been a good indication.

"I'll be out in a minute."

Jessica mumbled a prayer, putting her faith in whatever was out there that the redness in her eyes calmed. She pulled back the lock on the door and opened it.

"Have you been in here the whole time?" Sharon asked, her eyes narrowing.

Jessica thought it was best to lie to her. She didn't want her knowing that she was crying because of Jake. She could almost guarantee that "I told you so," would flow from her mouth at some stage.

"Of course not." Her tone was vulnerable, but she shook her head firmly as she made her way towards the sink. She stared at her reflection in the mirror and sighed quietly to herself when she didn't look even somewhat normal.

"Where were you then? I've been sitting in your office for the past hour."

Was she really gone so long?

But somehow, she doubted Sharon spent the last hour sitting in her office. Truly, she loved her best friend. They were more like sisters. But the woman had the attention span of a peanut. Sitting in an office for an hour doing nothing but looking at four walls would have driven her demented.

No, Jessica knew she was bluffing. She turned her head to look at her friend, whose face was plastered with guilt and something that quite scared her. She couldn't help herself, but Sharon's expression echoed with seduction. That forbidden lust dripping from her grey eyes. And there was a lot of forbidden. She exhaled deeply as she dried her hands.

"Were you really alone?" Jessica asked, raising her eyebrows sceptically.

Sharon stood still, silent for a long moment. Her fitted purple jeans moved with her curves as she shifted from one foot to another.

"Okay, maybe I wasn't in the office for long." She gave in, rolling her eyes. "I went on a brief trip to find you and I bumped into some cute guy."

"And which cute guy would that be?" Jessica laughed, tugging her friend out of the bathroom and out into the hallway towards her office. She was thankful for the subject change. If Sharon was good at anything, it was talking about herself.

"Some guy named Sam." She shrugged casually. "His mouth hit the floor when I spoke to him. Not because it was me, but just because I was female and speaking in his direction."

"No!" Jessica almost stomped her feet. "Not Sam. He's such a sweetheart. He does the coffee runs. Stay away from him, you man-eater. He's a child. He only started here. Leave him alone," she ranted, sitting in the soft leather chair at her desk.

He was twenty-three, so far from a child, but sit wasn't the point.

"Drama queen. He didn't look like a child from where I was sitting." Sharon crossed her arms, leaning back in her chair.

"Only you could come into a friend's job and flirt with the coffee guy. The poor boy is probably hyperventilating in the bathroom."

"That, or he's doing something else in the bathroom." Sharon laughed mischievously.

Jessica threw her hands up in defeat and grunted loudly.

"Ugh. You know what? I don't want to talk about it anymore. I have to work with him, and those mental images will not help."

"I agree. You changed the subject there for a minute."

She wanted to kick herself.

"Where were you? Were you in that cubicle all this time?"

"I needed to talk to Sophie about a few meetings I have lined up for next week," she answered, keeping Sharon's gaze.

For a moment, they only stared at each other. Sharon was searching her face for any evidence she was lying. She prayed that just this once, she could pull it off.

"And what happened with Jake? It looked pretty intense between you two."

"Nothing happened." She toyed with the hem of her blouse. "We just needed to get a few things straight."

"Like what?" Sharon pressed, and Jessica couldn't help but dart her eyes. Her friend's habit of wanting to know every detail played on her last nerve.

"Like nothing. I told him to stop fooling around with girls. He picks them up and drops them like a piece of shit, and I'm sick of working with his new secretaries."

Sharon tilted her head and glared. She had no idea what secretaries had to do with all of this.

"He sleeps with all of them," Jessica promptly informed her, sensing her friend's confusion. "Then they leave when they find out all he wanted was sex. I think I might put a warning sign on the notice board to say stay the hell away from him." Her blood boiled with anger, and her pulse quickened again.

"Are you jealous, Jess?"

"What is it with you people and thinking I'm jealous? I am not jealous. He just annoys the hell out of me," Jessica explained, taking a deep breath to calm herself.

"Well, there's something there, because I know you weren't talking to Sophie about your meetings. The first person I spoke to was Jake, looking like shit, by the way, and he said the last time he saw you, you were going into the bathrooms. An hour later, that is exactly where I find you."

"Why didn't you come for me then?"

"I figured you might have needed some time alone," Sharon replied, lowering her voice. "You let him in, didn't you?"

"No. If I did, it would've shattered me."

She was lying to herself again. She didn't want to open herself to the one man she was trying her hardest to hate.

And she was really trying.

"He's a great guy, Jess. He won't hurt you, and right now, you are only hurting yourself. You know he wouldn't hurt you. At least everyone else knows it." Sharon half-smiled. "He isn't Rob."

Jessica's mouth went dry at the mention of his name. She swallowed hard, letting the lump in her throat fade, fearing it would strangle her.

"I know he's not Rob. Of course, he's not—"

"You're scared," Sharon cut through. "I see it. I see it in your eyes that it scares you, and I could see the same thing when you were with that mongrel. You jumped when a man touched you. You still do."

Jessica's face was blank. A muted hatred flickered in her dead eyes. She hated being like this, and she hated others noticed.

Sharon was right. She couldn't bear the touch of a man. It was like an electric shock of pure fear. Rob may not have killed her, but he did an excellent job of deadening her emotions. She couldn't feel. She didn't want to. Not for him. He already took too much from her. He couldn't have this.

"But for some reason," Sharon went on, "this man that you are trying so desperately to hate, he's the only man you will allow to feel you in some way. He's the only one you are allowing yourself to be safe with. This past couple of months, I have watched the fear in your eyes when a guy came up to talk to you in a club. You freeze. To think of what he must have done to make you feel that much fear. I have no idea what it must have been like for you all those years you were with him."

Jessica watched as her friend's eyes filled with tears.

"He practically painted you black and blue for the best part, and nobody knew. I'll never forget that night when you came to my house. It was raining so heavily, and you were standing at my doorstep looking so helpless, hardly able to stand with blood running from your lip. Your whole body was full of cuts and bruises."

Jessica's tears stung her eyes as the memories forced themselves to the forefront of her mind.

"I could see you had enough. You couldn't take it anymore." Sharon wiped away the moisture dusting her eyes.

"I should have been stronger. I had plenty of chances to walk away and I didn't take them."

"Jess, you have no idea how strong you are. And you did walk away. Better late than never." Sharon glanced at her lap before looking up again. "I'm only bringing this up to remind you that Jake was there that night. I was having the get-together that you weren't *allowed* to attend. Jake dropped everything and ran to you. The world could have stopped, and he wouldn't have blinked. He did everything but tuck you into bed."

He did tuck her into bed.

"He was ready to go over there and beat the shit out of Rob, but you begged him not to."

Jessica hadn't forgotten. She chose not to remember. And it had nothing at all to do with Jake. It was a time involving Rob and the lowest point in her life. She didn't want to remember any of it.

"Remember when he used to call you every night to see if you were safe? Then you snapped and told him to stop bothering you and stop fussing over you." Sharon laughed, drying her face with her sleeve. "Start reading deeper into things, Jess. For two people that supposedly hate each other, he worries about you enough."

Jessica bit down on her full bottom lip to stop it from trembling. "I can't, Sharon," she finally spoke after a few moments of silence. "I just can't risk it. Not again."

"That's okay, sweetie. Take all the time you need. But I think I should warn you. I don't think Jake is going anywhere. Maybe you should try talking to him. And I don't mean blurting out your darkest secrets. That would make him run a mile." Sharon laughed inwardly.

"But talk to him. Be civil. Don't bite his head off like you usually do."

"Today was the first time I've bitten his head off in so long," Jessica defended.

"That's because you've been screwing him." Sharon was quick with the reminder. "Seriously, I bet it will surprise you if you do."

Jessica thought about it for a minute.

"Nope." She nodded her head. "Not going to happen. Me and Jake will never be. The only time we can have a civil conversation is when we are studying anatomy, and let me tell you, not much talking goes on then."

"Too much information."

"It's about time you had a taste of your own medicine." She eyed Sharon evilly, fighting the grin tugging at her lips.

With that, the two of them jumped as the phone rang loudly, echoing around the office.

"Hello," Jessica answered.

"It's Sophie. Mr. Williams left for the day. He wanted me to tell you there is paperwork on his desk for you. He said they were concerning the last project you did."

Nothing unusual. She loved her job, but it involved a lot of meaningless paperwork.

"Thanks, Sophie. Did he say why he was leaving?"

"I think he had a meeting. But between you and me, he left with Ciara," Sophie squealed.

Her heart fell into her stomach.

It shouldn't bother her. It shouldn't.

Ciara goes to these meetings to take notes, but it does little to ease the pain.

"Thank you, Sophie," she whispered before putting the phone back on the hook.

She went numb and her fingers gripped the arms of her chair as the pain built and built, powering its way to her fingertips. Right then, her heart tightened, and she cursed herself for asking anything at all.

NINE

Jessica stayed late at work that night, finishing the paperwork that was left for her. Her bones ached with stress and uneasiness, and the knots cramping her shoulders felt more like boulders.

She couldn't find an appetite since Sophie told her about Ciara and Jake's little rendezvous in the middle of the day. It made her sick to the bone to even think of it. Hating herself, she wondered where they were and what they were doing.

Scratch that thought. She knew exactly what they were doing. Where? Well, they had the entire city.

She yawned, feeling the tiredness seep through her like metal, making every inch of her feel heavy, sloppy, and downright uncomfortable. She piled the paperwork away before slipping her arms into her coat. The walk to the elevator felt more like a mile than a few steps, and the dim lighting of the hallway played on her struggling eyelids.

Coffee!

That's exactly what she needed. A nice cup of hot coffee to awaken her senses. She felt as though her body was going to crash at any minute. But as tired as she may have felt, she knew it was cruel of her to imagine she might sleep. She knew wishful thinking, and that was it. With what was swarming around her head, and would be long into the night, she knew closing her eyes to enter the dream-world was not a possibility.

She parked outside the nearest coffee shop, careful not to get her car door, or her legs, slated off as she got out onto the main road.

Walking inside, the smell of caffeine exploded through her in a wild torrent. Her mouth watered as the smell teased her tongue.

Tonight, she was going to be courageous with her choice of coffee. She felt spurred on by the thoughts of it passing her lips.

"Can I have a cappuccino to take away, please?"

A Cappuccino? It felt good to rebel.

"Jessica," she heard her name in the crackle of a deep voice.

She knew that voice, and the deep hum of his accent. She didn't move for a moment. Maybe she was imagining things. If she ignored it, would it go away?

"Jessica, is that you?"

Why wasn't his voice going away? Why wasn't *he* going away? The voice was persistent and caused shivers to scratch at her back. Her fingers twitched at her side, beating rhythms against her thigh.

She took a long, deep breath before turning on her heels, knowing she would dread the face she would see.

It was a year ago. She could do it. She would face him, feel absolutely nothing but hate, and storm right out of that coffee shop with her head held high.

How wrong she was. His dark, blank eyes locked with hers, connecting her to him. Recognition slammed her emotions. His blond hair was tightly cut and the stubble surrounding his thin lips was kept. A crooked smile edged up into his dimpled cheek.

Once upon a time, she loved that smile. She went weak at the knees from the adoration she oozed from seeing it. Now her legs solidified from fear.

"Rob," she breathed, feeling her heart thump faster.

She swallowed hard to get rid of the terror-soaked lump forming in her chest. It felt strange to feel something towards him again. All along, she experienced nothing but a numb heart for him.

Now?

She didn't know what it was, but she didn't like it. She was feeling something for him. Even if it was hatred, she didn't want it. She didn't want to waste emotion on him.

She loved this man for so long and there they were, standing face to face, no longer the happy couple they once were. Even if the happiness didn't last long.

He was her first love, and she knocked her head in ways to forget him, but she couldn't. It was impossible.

Only today, she fought tears speaking about him. What was it with her? Did she get a kick out of walking into disasters.?

Jessica Connors was a danger magnet.

"Your Cappuccino," the girl's voice interrupted their gaze, which between them, had progressed to more of a staring contest.

"Thank you." Jessica took the hot cup, letting the warmth caress her. She lowered her head. "I have to go."

"Wait," he called after her, locking his fingers around her wrist.

She gasped, feeling his touch.

"Sorry," he apologized, immediately dropping his hand, knowing he stepped a mile past the line. Her skin felt scorched. "Stay for a while."

He was playing a cruel joke on her, right?

"I… I can't," she stuttered, biting her tongue to halt her words. "I need to go. Sorry, Rob." She excused herself, hoping he would drop it.

"I've changed, Jess. Besides, it's only a chat. And better chatting here than in your apartment, don't you think?"

Her chest was trembling. Her lungs couldn't produce enough air to compensate for the fear, and the fractured breath she let out did little to ease the vibration in her stomach. He wanted her to know that he knew where she lived, and he would talk to her whether or not she agreed to it.

She also wasn't stupid. She knew—although he had claimed it—people like him never changed. They were always going to have it in them.

"Okay." She nodded, unwilling to let him intimidate her in her home. "Just for a minute, Rob."

The coffee shop was empty, but then so were the streets that were only occupied by tall streetlamps and drunks. It was raining outside, the drops pelted against the windows.

"You look good." He smiled. "Beautiful as always."

"What? Compared to the emotional wreck I was a year ago?" She couldn't help herself.

"I deserved that." He blinked, nodding his head.

"And much more, but I'm not here for that. I'm a firm believer in what goes around comes around and when it's your turn, it's going to come and bite you in the ass," Jessica snapped.

Counting to five, she shifted in her seat, looking up from her coffee after the liquid didn't pull her in and allow her to disappear.

"So, you're back? I thought you left to avoid everything?"

"I didn't leave to avoid things. I left because I needed to get away and realize exactly what I'd done. I needed to clear my head and think about things."

"And did the naughty step give you time to reflect?" she questioned sarcastically.

He dipped his chin. "It did. I loved you. I still love you and I pushed you away."

Jessica rolled her eyes, taking a sip from her cup.

"You didn't push me away. You kicked me away," she corrected him. "So much actually, I ended up with fractured ribs," she reminded him, taking pleasure in how he flinched when she said it. "Anyway, that's in the past. I've moved on. Hopefully, you have too," she told him, feeling the bitterness bubbling, settling at the top so that it could simmer.

"How's your family?" she queried, rooting for a change of subject. His family always made her feel so welcome, and everything that went on between her and Rob had nothing to do with them. She never blamed them; not when she loved them like her own.

"They're doing well. Michelle had a baby boy last week."

She was happy for her. Michelle was Rob's sister, and she was trying for a baby for several years.

"That's great."

"She's always asking about you. You should call her sometime."

"I'll do that," Jessica agreed, making a mental note to do so. They were close for the duration of her and Rob's relationship, but when she left, she lost all contact with Michelle. Never knowing exactly why. She put it down to awkwardness, not knowing what to say to each other after everything blew up.

She spoke to Rob for a while, and she managed to a hold a genuine conversation with him. She even laughed a little. The laughing reminded her of the good times they once had in their relationship. She forgot there were so many.

And for a while, she even wanted to believe he had changed. Not for her, but for the girl that would succumb to his ways next.

Then she remembered that he always was good at pretending. He practiced for three years with her.

"Oh, shit."

His dark eyes widened, and his head lowered towards the table.

"What are you doing?" Jessica questioned, her own eyes narrowing in confusion. He was hiding from something. No, not something, but someone. It was a nice reminder of the coward he really was.

What is going on with him?

"I wouldn't turn around if I were you," he advised. "If he sees you, we are both dead."

He shouldn't have told her not to turn around because her curiosity and the urge to do the exact opposite of what he said were too much. Turning in her seat, her face dropped. Jake's once soft chocolate pools were now hard and resembled iron. He was mad. Grinding his teeth, the muscles in his jaw ticked, and his broad shoulders squared, preparing for an attack.

"There's Jessica." Ciara pointed. The giggling blonde waved in her direction.

Out of all the places to bump into Jake, she did it sitting for coffee with the ex-boyfriend that instead of flowers, used to treat her to monthly visits to the hospital.

Her pulse quickened and pounded beneath her skin as he stalked towards their table.

"Look what we have here. Little reunion, is it?

"Jake!" Jessica warned, looking up at him under long lashes. His mouth set into a hard line.

"What the hell are you doing, Jess?"

"Nothing. We bumped into each other and had a chat."

What was she doing? She didn't need to explain herself to him.

"A chat? I really hope you are joking."

"This is none of your business. Keep out of it."

But he ignored her warning, turning his head to look at Rob, who was doing nothing to back down from this confrontation. He was indulging in it. She could tell from the hint of a smile threatening his lips.

"You piece of shit. I thought I made it pretty clear to you the last time to stay the hell away from her."

Shit, Jessica cursed. *This isn't good at all.*

Ciara stepped away from the situation, breathing in the scene playing out right in front of her, soaking it up for tomorrow's gossip story at the office.

"Jake, you always were such a great guy. Always doing your best to protect poor Jessica. Right now, she doesn't need your help, so back off." Rob planted his two feet firmly on the ground below him, standing to edge closer to Jake. Jessica watched as his hand balled into a fist at his side, ready to pounce when he needed it.

"Okay, will you two just stop it?" Jessica begged. "There is no need for this, and we were leaving. Weren't we, Rob?"

She darted a quick glance at him, hoping he would agree with her so she could get the hell out of there.

"Yeah, we were," Rob agreed.

The relief lifted a tonne of weight from her shoulders. Rob grabbed his black jacket from the chair, not once releasing his tight stare from Jake's eyes, then brushed past him and out of the coffee shop. She could tell by the raging expression on Jake's face that it took every ounce of his power not to punch him right there and have him plastered to the floor.

Rob was no match for Jake. Both were fit, but Jake was bigger. A lot bigger.

Jessica rushed out after him, not even daring to look back. She couldn't handle the guilt. She was a coward, but in times like this, she didn't mind.

"Rob, I think you should leave. I'm glad to hear you're doing well, but you and I meeting here and talking should have never happened, and you know it. Please go before any of this gets worse," she told him as she stepped outside onto the damp street. The mist was refreshing against her skin.

"If that's what you want, then I'll go."

"It is."

She didn't need Rob in her life anymore, in any shape or form. It was too dangerous. *He* was too dangerous.

He had disappeared when her name called out again.

"What?" she barked, spinning around. She was getting sick of being wrapped in cotton wool.

"Don't you dare do this to yourself again?"

"We weren't leaving together. He left by himself. Now, if you don't mind, I'm going home, and you can go back to screwing the blonde in there."

"Jess," he began, but she cut him off before he had a chance.

"Drop it. I know what you're going to say, so forget it and let me deal with it. I've had enough of this crap to last me a lifetime."

She stormed off, crossing the road to her car. He was still standing there, watching her as she drove away.

By the time she reached her apartment, her whirlpool of emotions had subsided to waves. She was angry, but had she the right? She was embarrassed and frustrated and extremely confused. She didn't know what to think anymore.

She gulped down a glass of water and closed her eyes for a moment, leaning her hands against the sink. The adrenaline from the past half hour kept her going, and it was still pumping through her blood. Or maybe it was the coffee.

Three loud bangs from behind her and her eyes shot open again, a fresh surge of energy running through her.

"Ugh, what now?" she grunted to herself.

She rushed to open it, not even thinking that it could have been someone dangerous. But as she would soon learn, the only danger she would face tonight was Jake as he barged into her apartment, his arms waving in the air.

"Where is he?" he blurted.

"You have got to be kidding me." Jessica threw her head back in frustration. "He's not here."

"What the hell were you thinking of letting him sit there with you like that, after everything he did to you?"

"Don't you think I know that?" she defended. "He hurt me enough. I wouldn't let him do that again."

"You were sitting there, laughing with him. It's sick to even think you would say hello to the scumbag but to entertain him with a conversation. I thought you knew better."

"How dare you? You don't know the first thing about what happened tonight, and you don't know shit about what I was thinking. What? You think after what he did to me, I was going to greet him with open arms. He scares the life out of me, Jake. I couldn't say no to him. Don't criticize me for something you know nothing about."

Tears were dusting her eyes, and she found herself having to bite down on her lip to stop it from trembling.

"Why didn't you call me if you were scared?" he questioned, as if it should have been the most obvious thing for her to do.

"I don't need you to protect me. I'm a grown woman. I can do things all by myself. I don't need you to hold my hand," she retorted, raising her voice a little, hoping it would get her point across.

"You would have left with him if I hadn't arrived. I could see it in your eyes."

What was he talking about? She had no intentions of going anywhere with him.

"After all this time, you still can't resist him, can you?"

Her breath caught in her throat, and her heart tightened inside her chest. She didn't realize words could hurt so much. She looked at him, her blue eyes looking like oceans under pools of tears. If she blinked, they would slide down her cheek; she could feel their heavy moisture.

"Get out!" she ordered, her voice weak as she let out a long breath.

"What?"

"Jake, get out of my apartment."

"Jess?" He approached her, reaching out towards her.

"Get out!" she screamed, feeling her sobs boil in her throat. "And this thing—whatever it is—that we have going on. It's finished. We can't keep hopping from bed to bed. You want to wrap me up and you also want to have sex with me. You can't protect me and screw me at the same time. And to be honest, I don't want you to do either. So, please, just get out of my apartment, and stop worrying about me, for Christ's sake."

"I can't stop. I don't know what it is with you, but I can't."

If Jake Williams had said that to any other woman, their hearts would have leaped right out of their chest, but not Jessica. She hated being cradled by people, especially him.

"I shouldn't have said what I said, but Christ, Jess, seeing you with him is making me go insane."

"Jake, please," she begged, gritting her teeth in anger. "It has taken me enough to build up the power to do this. Please don't test it because I will crumble and give in to you, and I'll hate you for it. Please."

Her energy was failing, and she knew if he questioned her once more, she would succumb to him.

"Then hate me, sweetheart. I'm not leaving. Not tonight."

"Get out! Get out! Get out!" she shouted, but instead of turning on his heels and walking out her door, he took three steps towards her, wrapping his arms around her trembling body. She fought against him so hard, hitting fists against his chest, but he wouldn't let her go, and she gave in to his strength because she knew she needed it.

“I don’t want you to hate me, but if you need to, go ahead. I’d rather be here with you while you hate me than anywhere else.” His expression was somber, his eyes soft, and the long kiss he placed on her forehead was tender.

She didn’t hate him.

Truth was, she never did.

Her sobs took complete control of her body, and words escaped that didn’t make sense.

“I’m sick, Jake,” she cried, but quickly realized the effect her words would have if she were to explain the full story.

“You’re sick?”

“Of this fighting,” she shortly corrected.

Her chest was rising and falling at frantic rates as her breathing was coming in heavy pants. His brown eyes melted against her ocean blues, and the spark exploded again. She recognized the longing in his eyes. It mirrored hers.

She lowered her voice somewhat and found the courage to speak the words she so desperately needed.

“Kiss me.”

Jessica bit down on her lip before he willingly obliged. His lips crushed against hers, moulding together perfectly. He laid her gently on the rug beneath them and locked his fingers tightly with hers as he raised her hands over her head, trapping her against him. She moaned against his kiss as his tongue explored her mouth, taking her in without even the slightest consideration for the fact that she was falling to pieces right there in his arms.

TEN

Jessica woke abruptly to a loud buzzing noise. Her unconscious brain did everything to block it out, but it continued until it dared her to open her eyes, haunting her ears with the cheap musical sound of sheer annoyance. She grunted loudly, pushing herself from Jake's warmth, reaching towards her bedside locker while hoping she wouldn't fall out of the bed. Lazily, her hand fumbled around, trying its best to find the irritating, flashing object without having to open her eyes.

She tapped the screen, and without saying a word, she put it to her ear, waiting for someone to say something.

"Hello, big boy." A seductive voice was on the other side. "Want to play?"

Jessica's eyes shot open. The gasp catching in her throat made her cough violently until she had to pound her palm against her chest.

"Excuse me? I'm sorry, but I think you have the wrong number." She swallowed.

"Ah, no, I don't," the voice demanded, sounding annoyed. She recognized that soft, high-pitched voice, but her tired mind wouldn't let her think.

"I'm sorry, but this isn't a hotline," she snapped. All she wanted to do was go back to sleep.

"Jessica?" the voice hushed, hesitantly saying her name. "Oh my God. Jessica Connors, is that you?"

"I should think so. You just called my phone. Who is this?" she commanded.

How could someone be so stupid? Who the hell did they think it was?

"First of all, it's Ciara, Jake's secretary."

Oh, so she did recognize the voice. She wasn't going totally mad. But why was she calling Jessica?

"And second, I didn't call you. I called Jake," Ciara stated bitterly.

Jessica's jaw dropped and blood rushed to her cheeks. Christ, how was she going to get out of this one?

She sprung her shoulders in the air, hearing Ciara give an impatient cough.

"How do you have Jake's phone? Do you swap phones often?"

Shit! Shit! Shit! You idiot. How can anyone be such an idiot?

"No. He… He left it here," Jessica lied, stuttering over her words.

"Don't give me that shit. I saw the way he ran after you earlier. He pushed me into a cab and took off after you. Does he like to take you on the side like some skank?"

Jessica was getting mad now.

"Okay, you listen here, Miss Peroxide. Yes, Jake came to see how I was, and yes, he left his phone here. Jake and I have known each other for a long time. But to be honest, this is none of your business, so I would appreciate it if you would keep your fake nose out of my life," Jessica spat, suddenly feeling awake.

"None of my business? I think it's my business. We slept together twice."

Lord. This poor girl was further gone than she originally thought.

Jessica cringed. She didn't want images of Ciara and Jake rotating like a slideshow in her head. No, thank you.

"Oh, my God. You're the reason he wouldn't touch me this weekend." She grew quiet. "I thought he just wanted to go slow. But I have a right to know if he is sleeping with someone else. I thought he was committed," Ciara screamed again.

So, she lied about their recent weekend together. Jake was telling the truth. Nothing happened.

Jessica tried awfully hard not to choke on hysterical laughter. "Commitment? Ciara, sweetie, word of advice: don't put commitment in the same sentence as Jake's name. It offends him." But she felt a sudden pang of guilt for Ciara. She may be going psycho with Jessica, but feelings aside, she didn't want to hurt her. "Did he say anything about you two dating?"

The line went silent for a long moment, and Jessica already knew the answer.

"No, not exactly," Ciara stammered, unable to find a coherent sentence.

"Ciara," Jessica began, but she cut her off.

The line went dead.

Jessica laid there with her ear still stuck to the phone. She felt sorry for her. She didn't deserve to be thrown around like a rag doll, and no one deserved to get hurt.

She switched off his phone and placed it on the locker, again mentally cursing herself for not opening her eyes before she had answered it.

She contemplated waking Jake to tell him what happened, but it was still dark. It was 2:30 a.m. She shifted around to face him, and the look on his face as he slept told her she couldn't wake him. He looked so peaceful and handsome, lying there as still as a marble statue with a body to match.

Quietly, she leaned over, kissed his forehead, and embracing the moments where she could make-believe he wasn't just with her for the sex. She was smiling as she closed her eyes to sleep again, the picture of his face engraved in her mind.

"Jess?" he whispered.

She opened her eyes again, feeling guilty for waking him. But when she did, his eyes were still closed.

Did he say her name in his sleep?

No, he would never.

No, not Jake.

For a moment, his face wrinkled under what looked like concentration. Then his eyes fluttered, a wide smile gracing his lips when they finally opened, staring straight into her soul.

"Now, there's a sight for sore eyes," he murmured, leaning in to kiss her softly on the lips. "Hello, beautiful." He winked with tired eyes as he backed away, resting his head on the pillow.

"Hello," she breathed, her eyes widening, taken aback by his spontaneous gesture. Then he did it again. She laughed to herself, wondering if he was still asleep.

"I should try that more often." He smiled that breath-taking smile. The one that caused her breath to catch in her throat.

"Okay." She beamed back, still looking astonished.

"You know what?"

"What?" she answered, searching his face for some evidence of what he was talking about.

"I'm going to do that again," he whispered, sounding serious.

Then he leaned in and kissed her. This time, he stayed there with his lips locked on hers. As they moved together, he edged closer, positioning her onto her back. His muscular arms caged her in at either side of her waist. His warmth hovered above her, making her want him even more. And as if he knew exactly what she was thinking, he deepened the kiss. Their passion radiated between them in a connection so powerful she was falling down a spiral of boiling lust. His tongue grazed her bottom lip. The intensity of his kiss caused her to lose herself in him until she didn't know who or where she was. She wrapped her arms tightly around his broad, muscular shoulders, keeping him there for support.

Jessica moaned as his lips left hers, travelled down her neck and back up again, kissing every inch of her face apart from her lips. It felt like her heart was leaping from her chest. He was kissing her so…. so different. Jake always kissed her passionately, but this felt completely foreign. It felt like he was cherishing every inch of her body until she completely succumbed to him. When his kisses stopped, she opened her eyes. He was staring down at her, both breathing frantically.

"Where did that come from?" she finally asked, out of breath and dizzy.

He stayed silent for a long moment

"I had this dream," he confessed, his eyes filled with pain. "I had a dream about you. You left."

Jessica swallowed hard to get rid of the lump forming in her throat. She wanted to say something, to assure him she wasn't going anywhere. But how could she make false promises?

"You're not going anywhere," he stated. "I won't let you."

She closed her eyes to stop the tears from falling. Then she pulled herself up on her elbows. They were so close she could feel his breath on her face, capturing her closer to him.

"If you say so," she whispered, and then she kissed him softly, permitting him to carry on where they left off.

***

The next morning, as Jessica tossed French toast on a plate, Jake emerged from the bedroom.

"There you are." He nodded at her. "I thought you sneaked off again."

"Nope," she chimed, smiling at him. "I had a craving for some French toast."

His eyes lowered to the plate in front of him.

"My favourite. You know I love you right now?" He laughed, leaning over to kiss her on the cheek.

"Yeah, yeah, shut up and eat," she ordered, smiling, and wondering why her entire body tingled when he said it.

"Oh," she blurted, swallowing her food. "I don't think you're going to have a secretary when you go to work today," Jessica informed him, secretly laughing to herself.

"What are you talking about?" Jake questioned, his brown eyes narrowing.

"Well, not only did you run off on her last night, but you left your phone on my locker."

"And what has that to do with anything?"

"When someone calls at 2 a.m., I don't really open my eyes to check if I'm answering *my* phone. It was yours, and it was Ciara. The poor girl had a hissy fit."

Jake laughed loudly as she explained everything to him, shaking his head in disbelief.

"She called me a skank. I'll show her how much of a skank I am." Jessica raised her eyebrows, feeling the anger boil, which only made Jake laugh even harder. "So, yes, I don't think you'll have a secretary this morning."

"And you expected her to believe that I left my phone here? Get real, baby. She's a smart girl."

"It was the best I had. I wasn't going to tell her I slept with you. She would have been around here with a gun and a shovel."

"You always had an active imagination. But she won't leave."

"How do you know?"

"How could you leave this face?" He pouted. "It's irresistible."

"You are so full of shit, Jake Williams." Jessica threw a piece of toast at his face.

"Oy! Just because you're hot doesn't mean you can get away with throwing food at me." He used his voice of authority; a voice Jessica could never take seriously.

"Shut up and eat, Jake!"

Later that morning, she sat in her office, sipping on her coffee as she replied to emails.

"My secretary quit," Jake stated, suddenly appearing, leaning against her door frame.

"Hate to say it, but I told you so. She could resist the face after all." She felt rather proud of herself for being right.

"And she left one hell of a rumour in her wake. I heard our names being mentioned at least five times on the way down here."

"Great! That's just great. Where did I get you from?" Jessica threw her head back, hoping someone out there would give her an answer because right now, she had no idea.

Men! she thought to herself.

"I need a new secretary," Jake told her, shrugging casually, knowing he could have his pick of sexy blondes. He didn't even care about the rumours.

Jessica grunted in distaste. "You know I'm being called the office slut out there and you want a new "

"You're not being called a slut. They know you're not. They love you around here. Believe me, they don't think about you. They only want something to talk about, and unfortunately, we are today's bait, but you know how they are. It will calm down after today."

She knew he was right, but it still didn't make her feel any better. Jessica didn't want everyone to know she was sleeping with her boss. He may have been Jake to her, but to everyone else, he wasn't. He was the powerful man upstairs who decided exactly how far you could go in this company.

"Just relax, Jess," he advised, turning his gaze to the window.

He always loved Jessica's office. He loved the view of the city, watching the people below. From his office, you were closer to God than the ground and the people below looked like ants. With him being the boss, she didn't know why he didn't take it from her. He could if he wanted.

"Jake," she called after giving him his few minutes.

"Uh-huh?" he answered, turning his head to look at her.

Damn that man! She couldn't even look at him, and her stomach started doing gymnastics.

"Do me a favour?" she asked.

"Anything your heart desires."

"Get your ass out of my office."

"I'm your boss. I can stay here if I want."

"No, you can't. It's harassment. Besides, I'm also the woman you are screwing, so unless you want to keep on using that drill of yours, I would do as I say," she demanded.

"Wow," he breathed. "It turns me on when you're feisty."

"Then turn yourself off. I'm busy. Please get out," she practically begged. She knew if he sat there any longer, she would get nothing done, and she had a lot to do.

"You'll be busy later," he promised before he left.

"Yeah, that's what you think," she shouted after him.

Seriously, who was she trying to convince? She was a terrible liar, even to herself.

"Nope. I can't leave yet," Jake disagreed, strolling back. She threw her pen on the table and looked at him with evil eyes. He was beginning to annoy her.

"Why?" she shouted her moans.

"Just because." He shrugged, walking closer and closer until he was standing right in front of her, wedged between her legs.

She eyed him suspiciously, wondering why the hell he was standing in front of her like that. But then she gasped inwardly, feeling his warm hands cradle her face. When she looked up again, she could feel his cool breath on her face, and his eyes staring right into hers. He leaned in even closer and kissed her hard on the lips. Lingering there for a moment longer, she sighed like a teenage girl.

Then he straightened and walked away, leaving a dumbfounded Jessica behind him.

ELEVEN

She slipped her long arms into her knee-length coat and made her way towards the coffee shop across the street. The wind that swept across her bare legs was moist and stung with a bitter chill. Winter was here. She could smell it in the air, and she loved it.

What was it about winter that instantly brought the images of flaming fires, snuggled up with a cosy blanket and a hot cup of cocoa? How could it not be people's favourite part of the season?

"Jess!"

She spun around, the wind making her loose, dangling curls stick to her face. The sight of Jake running towards her, his grey suit fitting perfectly to his toned body, made her pulse quicken.

"Where are you going?" he questioned, catching up with her.

"I'm going to get coffee."

"Mind if I come?"

"No." A smile graced her full lips.

Taking a step inside the heated coffee shop, the warmth made her cold cheeks tingle.

"Go sit down," he told her before making his way towards the counter.

Strange. For once, he wasn't flirting with the girl behind the counter. She looked disappointed.

"What was the face for?"

She hadn't realized it, but she was looking at him funny. Her face was tight, her eyes narrowing, and nose wrinkled into something painful.

"Sorry, I'm in one of my daydreams," she lied, looking away, hiding the fact her face was turning pink.

"I thought you should know's a new guy starting today," he said, taking a gulp of what Jessica suspected was tea.

"Really? Who?"

"Our new publishing executive. He gets in at two, so I was hoping you could show him around. He transferred here from JK's Publishing House."

"That's hot. You know what they say about the men over there in JK's Publishing House?" Jessica's eyes sparkled.

"Claws off, tiger," Jake warned, laughing. "It's against company policy to sleep with a colleague."

"It looks like you will have to handcuff me and throw away the key."

"Any time, baby."

Jessica rolled her eyes, shaking her head in disgust. She should have known he was going to say something like that. "There really is no stopping you, is there?"

He agreed with a smug nod.

For a long moment, they sat there in silence, both listening to the havoc surrounding them. When she thought about it, their shared silence was never awkward. It was comfortable, as if they were both content to sit in each other's presence and not decode unspoken words.

When she turned her head to look back at him, he was staring straight at her; his dark, coffee-coloured eyes melting her. She looked away in fear she would get lost in his gaze.

"Jake?" Her voice was low, looking out onto the street where people were rushing.

"Yes, sweetheart?"

Jessica tilted her head to look at him again, only this time, he was smiling slightly.

"What do people do if time is running out?" she asked, knowing it was a risky question, but she needed his answer. "When they want to live every minute of their lives before it's too late?"

For a minute, he searched her face for some sort of explanation. Then he rubbed his fingers over the bridge of his nose.

"You're asking me? Were you not the very girl who told me she lived every day as it comes?"

"Yes," Jessica agreed, nodding her head. "But I don't think I'm doing it right."

"Jess?" His face drenched with concern as he reached over to take her hands in his.

Instead of answering him, her eyes were begging, pleading with him desperately. She didn't know why it mattered so much to her, but she needed to know what he would do.

Jake swallowed hard, and the tension in his face eased.

"You fight every day," he answered honestly. "Five years ago, when my mother was dying," he began, "I watched her fight every day when she was sick. Every day was a struggle against the evil inside her. But she fought, and she kicked and screamed until she felt she had won. She fought it out until the bitter end and until she didn't want to be a winner anymore. The doctor gave her four months. A year later, she was still pottering around."

Jake had always taken his mother's death extremely hard. That was why she was so scared of letting him in. She didn't want him to go through any of it again. It would kill him.

"When she was dying," he continued, "I've never seen so much love come from one person in all my life. She told me to enjoy life the way I thought I should. She told me to find the woman I love." Jake's eyes faltered from Jessica's face, onto the table where his features narrowed into a sudden concentration. It was like he was realizing something for the first time.

Jessica breathed in softly as his warm hands tightened around hers.

"She told me that when I find that girl, to never let her go and fight like hell until she's mine."

But then he sharply pulled his hands away and gazed out onto the street. "All I have to do now is find someone worth fighting for." He shrugged coldly.

The colour drained from her face, an icy chill making her shudder. She cursed herself for feeling this way. She wasn't supposed to get attached like this. Wasn't this everything she warned herself about, everything she told herself wouldn't happen?

She sipped away the last drop of her coffee while checking her watch.

"I think we should get going," Jessica announced, standing and grabbing her coat.

Jake agreed, jumping up, smiling as if he had said nothing at all.

And why would he? He was being honest. He hadn't found the person worth fighting for yet, and as much as it killed Jessica to admit, she needed to get over it.

***

Jessica blinked her heavy lids over glossy eyes and smothered back the urge to yawn as she stood limp, shredding paper. It was amazing how she always became so easily amused. It was now two in the afternoon, and she was standing over the shredder for the past hour, watching as the tiny swords inside the electrical machine sliced through the delicate paper like a lion who hadn't hunted in weeks. Its steel claws roared to life as each white sheet merely touched the entrance.

She needed a night out on the town with alcohol, high-heels and a dance floor. That's all she wanted in her simple life. It beat shredding paper half the afternoon.

But there was a reason she was tired and lazy. After Jake lost his last secretary, which, to be fair, was partly her fault, she had agreed to hold interviews for the new position, and she found the perfect match. She was quite pleased with her choice. They were smart, clever, and particularly good-looking.

"Good morning."

"Speak of the devil," she muttered.

He tilted his head to look at her with suspicious eyes. Did she look that bad?

"What are you doing shredding paper in your bare feet?"

"My carpet is really soft, Jake. You should try it. And please don't ask about the paper shredding. There is something about the noise that calms me."

"How long have you been standing there?" His gaze was scrutinizing. Maybe she was going mad.

"An hour," she answered with no shame, still standing there lazily, balancing on one leg as she tried to scratch it with her other foot.

"Have you nothing better to do than stand there and give yourself paper cuts?"

"I have plenty to do. I just don't want to."

He accepted her answer without argument. How could he argue

with her now? She was even too lazy to bend over and scratch her leg with her fingers. If he tried an argument, she was simply going to blink in response.

Epic!

Energy? That disappeared when her coffee from this morning drained from her system. She was now on autopilot, and the battery was slowly dying.

"You always were the definition of class, Jess, you know that?" She merely yawned in response.

"How did the interviews go? I hope you came across as more enthusiastic than you are now?"

"I found a new assistant. Great references and plenty of experience."

"Fantastic! What is she like?"

"Blonde, blue eyes, glorious body."

That got his attention.

"And male," she continued.

"Male?"

"A very gay male," she went on.

His eyes widened.

"What's wrong with you? You wanted a new assistant, not a personal stripper, and I got you a rather wonderful assistant. Don't complain about his sex. Give him a chance. I guarantee he will do well."

He paused for a moment, obviously contemplating whether to let her away with this one.

He smiled. "Thank you."

A light tap on the door had their heads spinning.

Jessica watched as Jake rose from his seat, stretching out his hand to whoever was on the other side.

"Mark, good to see you again."

Quietly, she popped her head around, nosily breathing in the scene. But her eyes did an unnatural wonder of the man standing in view.

A tall, ruggedly handsome being, shaped out in a black suit, smiled down towards her. Composing herself, she stood up straight, brushing down the creases in her skirt before she crept around the door to greet him.

"Jessica Connors, it's a pleasure to meet you." She extended her hand.

"Mark Walters. The pleasure is all mine."

"Jessica will show you around if you'd like?" Jake offered.

"That would be great. If you're not too busy?" Mark glanced towards her.

"Believe me," Jake butted in. "She's not busy."

Jessica eyed him unappreciatively. She didn't like people answering for her. But considering she was shredding paper for the last hour, showing Mark around would be like an adventure.

"It's no problem. Come with me."

She walked a few steps ahead before realizing the ground was still incredibly soft.

"Shit," she whispered to herself, feeling the blush rise in her cheeks, looking down at her bare feet. And turning around only made matters worse as both Jake and Mark were both staring at her, trying their best to hide the laughter.

"Maybe it's best if I put my shoes on before I take you anywhere." She smiled, releasing the tension for them both to chuckle.

"Yes, that may be a good idea," Mark agreed.

As Mark and Jake shook hands and said goodbye, Jessica finally started showing the new guy around. This time with her shoes on.

"As you can probably tell by all the photocopying machines. This is the photocopying room."

"Exciting place."

"You think it's exciting now? Come in here before a deadline when all the machines are in overdrive. The buzz gets your adrenaline pumping," she joked. "And word of advice, if you ever want to photocopy your ass, just let people know. It's no problem. We're fine with that kind of stuff around here, but it's good to let people know so we don't walk in on you, because there is nothing more awkward than walking in on someone sitting on the machines."

He laughed loudly, his broad shoulders shaking under his suit. "It's good to know."

"Let's move on." She continued walking along the corridor towards the kitchen.

"I'm guessing this is where everyone has sex." He ran his fingers through his fair coloured hair.

"You've got it. Just don't tell anyone about the sex. We don't mind walking in on that."

"So, you're those kinds of people."

"What kind of people would that be?" she questioned, her eyes narrowing.

"The perverted kind."

She paused for a moment, her eyes wandering from him, towards the kitchen and back again.

"I prefer open-minded, but if that's what you want to call it."

"It's good to know I'm working with someone with a sense of humour."

"Oh please, you got me on a good day. I'm a complete bitch most of the time."

"Thanks for the warning." He nodded.

For the next twenty minutes, she guided him around the floor, making silly jokes and introducing him to the rest of his colleagues, finally ending back at Jessica's office.

"Take a seat." She gestured, seating herself down behind her desk.

As he slipped off his jacket and sat back in the chair, Jessica couldn't help but notice his muscular arms. What was it about a man's arms that got her heated every time?

"Do you have a family at home, or are you married to your work like most of us in this building?"

"I have two kids at home."

"They're beautiful," Jessica said as she pressed her fingers along the photos he had taken out of his wallet. A boy and a girl, both stunningly beautiful with Mark's enviable features: fair hair with the same deep violet eyes, and dimples on their left cheek.

"I'm a lucky man," he stated proudly.

Jessica admired that. She wanted a family someday, but what you want and what you can have are two different things.

"You are," she agreed, sounding firmer than she felt. "How about a wife, or girlfriend, or both?" She giggled openly.

"I was married. Technically, I still am. I'm separated from my wife. She's going through a hard time right now. I'm helping her through it. We're still best friends."

Now she felt stupid, and the knot in her stomach churned.

"I'm sorry. I didn't mean to pry."

"Don't be silly. We've been separated for a while now. The kids are fine with it. That's all that matters."

"No girlfriend then?" she queried. Honestly, her desire to know other people's business made her own life seem pathetic.

“I’ve been thinking about getting back out there for a while. It’s a big step.”

“You should. Women in this city are crying out for a man like you.” Jessica’s lips edged up into a soft smile.

This guy was nice. Really nice.

But when she closed her eyes for a moment, he wasn’t the face she saw in her fantasy.

TWELVE

The rest of the week went by quickly, and she spent her weekend relaxing—for once. She spent the previous weekends with Jake.

As much as she hated to even think about it, his comments in the coffee shop on Wednesday pained her deeply. She knew she shouldn't have noticed. It was Jake Williams, for Christ's sake. Why would he fall in love with her? She continued to remind herself of that. Otherwise, she'd curl up into a ball, and that wouldn't help.

Jessica shook her head, letting her negative thoughts go. She didn't need it, not today. Today was Monday and her appointment kept edging closer. She hated her doctor's appointments. The news was getting worse with each visit.

She booked the day off from work, deciding not to go through Jake and run it by Mr. Johnson instead.

It would bring up too many questions.

Still, she was fooling herself if she thought she was getting away with it that easily. It was eleven o'clock and any minute, she was expecting a call from him. Surely, he would miss teasing her about their sex life by now.

Jessica cringed. She couldn't believe they even had a sex life.

A fling?

She could get over that because it's a once-off thing. That's exactly what it should have been. She should have stopped it after she was sneaking out of his house and leaving her underwear behind. But no.

Jessica Connors hates making her life simple.

Instead, she made their sex-fling into a sex-life.

"I need to get a normal life. One with no complications," she murmured to herself as she plopped herself on the sofa.

As she did, her phone flashed like she expected.

"Right on time," she whispered.

"Williams," Jessica answered, knowing exactly who was on the other end.

"Why are you at home? Are you sick?" Jake questioned.

"Are you checking up on me?" She chewed on the crisps she had taken from the cupboard. "Worried about me, are we?"

"I'm your boss. You're not at work. I should know why."

"I told Tony."

"Tony Johnson would bend over and kiss your feet if you asked him to."

She shudders.

"Would you?" she teases.

"I'd prefer to bend you over."

This man.

She huffed, brushing the crumbs from her lap.

"Should I always come through you for a simple day off? As you said, you're my boss. Bosses don't need to know everything about their employee's personal lives." Jessica clicked her tongue against the roof of her mouth.

"Calm down."

"Don't tell me what to do."

For a moment, the line went silent.

"Jess, are you okay?" Jake finally spoke.

"I don't know," she breathed, feeling confused. Her mind felt blurred. Maybe it was nerves. "You're driving me crazy. I might have slept with you, but I can't tell you everything. You need to stop playing the *you-slept-with-me-and-I'm-your-boss-so-you-have-to-do-as-I-say* card. Just give it a break. Please," she begged.

"Okay," Jake agreed, his tone becoming suddenly different. "I don't mean to play that card with you, and I don't expect you to do everything I say. I saw you weren't at work. I thought something was wrong. You never miss work."

Jessica rolled her eyes. Now she just felt guilty for snapping at him.

"There's nothing wrong. I promise. I have a check-up at the

doctor."

"Everything okay?"

"It's all good. I'm going to get some medication for those headaches." Jessica bit down on her lip, hoping he wouldn't hear more in her voice.

"You should do that."

She sighed with relief. He usually knew when she was lying. Maybe she didn't want him to know so much that she was getting good at lying to people about it.

"Anyway, I should be off. I'm going to be late for the appointment. I'll talk to you tomorrow."

"Good luck at the doctors."

They both said goodbye and hung up. She should've taken pleasure in snapping at Jake, but she didn't.

She hated being confused.

On the way to the hospital, she couldn't help but flick her eyes towards the digital clock on the dashboard—every minute bringing her closer to her appointment.

Jessica gave her details to the nurse at the desk and waited patiently for someone to call her name.

"Jessica Connors."

She turned her head towards the booming voice where the smiling face of her doctor greeted her.

"Jessica, how are you?" Doctor Harris grinned widely, exposing his slightly crooked teeth. His eyes were smiling at her too, and the dark wrinkles that were set around his eyelids became deeper. His grey hair was thinning, and his brilliant white shirt looked like it was hanging on for dear life, hardly buttoned on his rounded belly.

"I'm good. Thank you."

As she sat opposite him with only the desk separating them, that overwhelming feeling of fear and unease caressed her again.

Jake!

He was the first person to jump into her head. He protected her from things like this, and she wanted him near her. For the first time, she didn't want him because of the passion between them or the sex. She wanted him because he could make her feel safe with just a touch of his hand.

"How have you been feeling, Jessica?" the doctor interrupted her thoughts of longing.

She took a deep breath before she spoke. "I've been good so far. Some migraines. Nothing too serious."

"That will be the medication." He nodded while taking the brown chart from under a pile of papers.

Her heart beat viciously in her chest. It surprised her it wasn't echoing around the office, bouncing against the blue painted walls as a reminder of why she was here.

Jessica knew what the chart held: the results of her tests. She already knew what was wrong with her, but those test results told her exactly how bad it was.

"As you know, we have run multiple tests and scans on you throughout the last few weeks. The cold coagulation treatment we did on you—its purpose was to stop this disease from spreading. But we compared the results of the biopsies we took in August to the test we did on you three weeks ago, and our treatments aren't working."

Jessica blinked away the tears forming in her eyes and swallowed the lump threatening to choke her.

"Okay," she said, trying her best to digest his words. "I was preparing myself for that."

"I'm going to give it to you straight up, Jessica. I have been your doctor for a while, and you seem like a girl who can take it. You have stage two adenocarcinoma. It's an invasive cancer. I would like to do a full hysterectomy or a combination of radiation and chemotherapy. I can't promise it won't be both. It's not sweet. This is tough. Cervical cancer is no simple task for any woman to deal with, especially one who doesn't already have children."

"Is there any way I would be capable of having children afterwards? Are there any options for that?"

"With a hysterectomy, we can take the cancer before it spreads, but there is no chance of you ever carrying your own child. With chemotherapy and radiation, there is a slight chance, but it's near impossible you could have children afterwards. It may stop your ovarian activity completely."

For weeks and weeks, she asked herself, why me? Until she finally realized it had to happen to someone.

When Jessica turned twenty-five, she was called for her first cervical check. It took her two years to find the time in her schedule to organize her appointment. She didn't know then it would lead to countless doctor's appointments and biopsies.

Her dignity ran away with the first piece of tissue they cut from her cervix, and her first colposcopy shamed her to cry. She thought it would be better to have a female gynaecologist. But as she soon learned, it didn't matter if it was an alien. They were still sitting between her legs as if it were the most natural thing to do, prodding her with metal instruments.

That was the day the word biopsy was first mentioned. She couldn't believe it. A biopsy had to mean something bad, didn't it? Then came the news she would have to wait six long, excruciating weeks for the results.

When she did finally get the phone call, she didn't cry. She laughed. She laughed so hard she vomited. And to slap her a little harder, they told her it was a very slow-growing disease. How long had this evil been nesting inside her?

A week later, her first treatment began. The violent shaking from the anaesthetic, and the smell of her burning flesh, caused acid bile to settle in her throat.

And here she was, sitting in a dull doctor's office, once again shattering her world with more bad news. She was twenty-seven. She had a life to live. She thought it would include children. Life is a journey of unexpected hardships and agony. It was up to her to fight it. To kick that life in the ass and build her own.

"Which one is less noticeable?" she finally asked, shifting in her seat. She hated talking about this, but it needed to be done.

Doctor Harris' gaze deepened. The wrinkles around his eyes looked carved into his skin, and his thin lips pursed into a pout. She knew he thought it was a stupid question, but she had to ask it. He pushed his slipping glasses back onto the bridge of his nose and stared at her for a while longer. She kept his gaze, refusing to look away.

"The hysterectomy would be less noticeable," he answered, worried. "With the other treatments, there will be hair loss and weight loss. I mean, people will know you are sick, Jessica."

"I know. But with the hysterectomy, it could be any operation. I don't want to suffer for months, even years on end because of this. If I get my womb out, it will be over and done with within a few weeks, and I can get back to what I was doing." She sounded cold, and she hated it. It killed her to say those words, but she couldn't let it sink in. If she did, the emotional pain alone would kill her.

Jessica wanted a family. She wanted kids to play with, to snuggle into bed at night. Unfortunately for her, it wasn't meant to be. And if she was being honest, it also killed the feelings she had for Jake. Not because she didn't want to feel anything for him, but she couldn't. Not anymore. She knew how much he loved kids.

"Jessica, does anybody know you are ill?" It was like Doctor Harris had made a sudden realization.

She hoped he wouldn't ask.

"No," she answered honestly, lowering her eyes to her lap, where her hands were fumbling with a tread she had pulled from her top.

"Jessica, you need to tell someone. You can't go through this alone."

"I won't," she assured him.

"You need to tell somebody. It doesn't matter which line of treatment you decide to take, you are still going to need someone there to take care of you."

"I will tell someone. I promise."

She wanted to beg him to change the subject.

"Please do, because you will need all the help you can get. For now, I'll prescribe you some more medication and something for those headaches. But I want you to go home and have a think about what you are going to do."

"But I already know," she interrupted.

"You might think you know now, but I want you to leave your options open. Don't make a rash decision you might regret. I will book you in for an MRI and ultrasound next week. By then, we can have things set up. Take a week to decide and let us know. I know when people think of cancer, time isn't one of the major factors, but this is the most crucial part, and you need to know you are doing the right thing. So, go home and think about it. And tell somebody," he warned.

"Okay." She nodded, letting a single tear fall. She felt numb. And that's how she wanted it. If she wasn't numb, she would feel all the pain, and it would come crashing down on her like a tonne of bricks.

"We will call with your next appointment. But please, if you are ill, or you just want to talk and find out more information, don't hesitate to call me. You have my phone number. Use it."

"Thanks, Doctor Harris." Jessica smiled, wiping away the moisture from her cheeks.

As she left his office, she looked at her watch. It was 1:30. She knew where she wanted to go. She may have taken the day off, but she was going to work. Not to read or edit books, but Jessica needed to be with the man who protected her most.

She needed Jake, whether or not she liked it.

THIRTEEN

Jessica's heavy tears caressed her skin as she parked her car in the parking lot outside the company building. Her drops felt like bricks as they lulled at her cheeks and splattered onto her lap.

"Breathe," she told herself, wiping away the mascara-soaked tears. She knew she couldn't walk into work looking like this. But her longing to be with Jake threatened to cripple her if she didn't get to him.

Walking swiftly inside the building, head to the floor to remain unseen, she rushed straight for the ground floor restroom. She splashed some water on her face and wiped away the tears. Luckily, the red and blotchy patches on her face were less noticeable now.

On the way up, she asked herself what the hell was she going to do? What was she thinking? But immediately said to hell with logic. It was way past the point for rational thinking. People were looking. They'd seen her already. Jake would hear about her visit eventually.

Stepping out of the elevator, she felt her heart thumping against her chest like it was about to explode. Taking a deep breath, he forced one foot in front of the other and walked swiftly down the hall towards his office. She had no idea what she was going to do or say, but she was gone too far to turn back now.

No light filtered through from his office. It was closed. Hand on the door handle, her heart in her mouth, she twisted, that same heart slowly sinking back into her chest when she finds the room empty.

"He went out, sweetheart." Margaret approached, startling her from behind, a small smile gracing her wrinkled lips. Margaret worked in accounts on the same floor for many years before Jessica started her job.

"Oh." Jessica sighed, feeling a pang of disappointment.

"He should be back soon. I think I heard he had a meeting on the other side of town. Would you like me to take a message?"

"No, it's fine. I was just popping by." Jessica waved her hand in dismissal. With luck, Margaret wouldn't even tell Jake she was there.

"Just popping by." Margaret whispered.

"Excuse me?"

"I don't think Jake would see it as just popping by."

"What?"

Jessica watched as Margaret shifted from one foot to another.

"I've known you for a long time. And even though I haven't been working for Jake all that long, I think I know him a little. You don't have to be stupid to see he can have any girl he wants. He relishes in it. But he looks at you differently. I don't know what it is, but it gives me goosebumps when two of you are together." She smiled. Her frail voice had a droned quality to it, as if all her words were attached. "And not fighting," she quickly added.

Jessica looked at her for a moment, unable to find the words to respond. How was it that everyone else could see what was going on between her and Jake as something special? She didn't know what it was exactly, but she couldn't.

"I think you need stronger glasses, Margaret," Jessica joked, trying her best to avoid the subject.

"There is absolutely nothing wrong with my glasses, little girl. It is you that needs glasses. Open your eyes. You will see it too."

"I'm now walking away from this awkward conversation and going to go to my office."

Jessica hugged her lightly, afraid she would break a bone in the woman's fragile frame.

"I know what I'm talking about," Margaret shouted after her.

"No, you don't."

Jessica heard her mutter something under her breath as she walked away, but she didn't catch it.

She was here now. She decided to stay and catch up on her work. She tried to ignore the conversation she just had, put it to the back of her mind and hope it would stay there, but she couldn't do it. She had butterflies, excitement building through her shoulders. She hated those butterflies. She wished they would roll back up into their cocoons, exactly where her feelings were hiding.

Her eyes flickered to a figure rushing past her office. A few moments later, he backtracked his steps. Jake looked at her, confused, a smile playing on her lips as he slowly opened the office door, and stood there, a bemused look on his handsome face.

"You are insane, woman," he breathed, nodding his head in disbelief. "I should have known you wouldn't stay away."

Her heart beat madly. That feeling was there. The one she was yearning for. It was the reason she came to work. It felt like her heart had travelled up into her mouth and wouldn't let her speak. That man did weird things to her. But she wanted his touch. The touch that was silently killing her but spoke volumes about how it would protect her.

"Why are you at work, Jess? You took the day off."

"I had things to do," she explained.

"Everything good? How did the doctors go?"

"I'm fine," she demanded. "Change the subject, Jake."

He sighed in defeat. "Guess what we are doing for the weekend?"

"Each other?" She raised her eyebrows in question.

"We're doing that too. But it's not what I meant." He put his hand in his pocket and pulled out a small gold card. "Collins and Jones' Agency is holding their famous gala. And you," he poked her nose, "Are my date."

An infectious smile spread across her face as she leaned back in her chair, folding her arms.

"Am I now?" She plucked the invitation from his hand, studying the all too fancy black decorated writing. Shouldn't she be throwing a hissy fit now? Screaming at him for deciding for her?

"You are." He smiled, gently caressing her bare shoulder where her knitted jumper had fallen.

She shivered under his touch and looked up at him through feathered lashes. Right now, she was too damn stupid to scream at him, too taken away with his body close to hers.

"So, you're going to get a pretty dress and be your beautiful self, and I will be a very proud man to have you by my side."

"That's more like it."

Jake pecked her nose, pressing lightly.

"I'm not finished. Then I'll bring you back to my place, where that beautiful dress will look even prettier on the floor."

Jessica rolled her eyes and exhaled loudly. "I should have been expecting that," she told herself, lowering her head to hide the blush burning under her skin.

"I was thinking," Jake began, laughing at her comment. "We will go to the party Saturday night. We will have sex afterwards, but we could have sex now, too." His mischievous eyes shining with trouble.

"My table is awfully small."

"My bed isn't."

"Later, sweetie. Later." She nodded, patting his chest. He sighed heavily and leaned closer to her.

"Okay, beautiful, but for now, I'm just going to kiss you."

And before she knew it, he locked his lips with hers.

FOURTEEN

"Do you honestly believe he loves you?"

The sun beat its rays down on her skin, making her head thump.

"What?"

She was on a busy street, but she had no idea where.

And where was the voice coming from?

"Get real, Jessica. Jake has had many women. What makes you think you are any different?" The voice continued in her ear, making her heart pound with pain. "Look." The smooth voice directed her towards the other side of the street, where Jake was walking hand in hand with someone.

Another someone.

It wasn't her.

"He doesn't look like he is thinking about you now."

Jessica couldn't help the feeling that her heart sunk into the pit of her stomach, sending bile to her throat.

She recognized the fair-haired beauty that had her hand clasped in his. It was Katie. His ex. The one who broke his heart.

They dated since they were both seventeen. At twenty-five, after eight years together, Jake asked her to marry him, and she accepted. They were the fairy-tale couple everyone aspired to be. That was, until Jake walked in on her with another man two years after the engagement.

Still, seeing him smiling at her like that made Jessica's blood boil with jealousy.

And why the hell was she with him? His luring eyes glistened as he stared down at her.

"Doesn't he look so in love?" The voice continued to nag, and it continued as her eyes filled with bitter tears. "He doesn't look too worried about you. Then again, why would he? Look at her. Look at you. The difficulty to decide."

Her throat tightened and the hot wetness trailed down her cheeks.

"Besides, you won't be here for much longer. You're dying. And if you really love him, you will want him to be happy."

"Of course, I want him to be happy," Jessica agreed, her breathing becoming frantic as the beads of sweat slid over her collarbone. She wanted to scream as she watched Jake reach in closer to Katie's lips. A wide, loving smile spreading across his beautiful face.

The street began to spin as he reached in even closer.

Then everything went black.

***

Jessica sat up sharply, feeling her heart pound viciously against her chest. The cold sweat seeped through her pores. She hated dreams like that. They were always too real, and every time she got them, it was for a reason. She didn't even want to think about why she had this one.

A loud bang made her jump once again. This time it was her front door. Giving her pulse time to calm, she climbed out of the bed and through her living room towards the door. She opened it cautiously, still panicking from her dream, and sighed with relief when Sharon's irate face greeted her.

"What is with the face that launched a thousand ships?" Jessica grunted as her friend stood there with her arms firmly crossed.

"Hilarious. Do you know how long I've been standing out here waiting for you to answer the door? It's one o'clock in the day. What the hell are you still doing in bed?" Sharon yelled, storming into the apartment with her arms flying about.

"One o'clock?" Jessica repeated, astonished she had stayed in bed for so long.

"Yes, one o'clock and I'm hopelessly hungover, so it's not the best day to have me standing outside your front door waiting for you to answer."

"You have keys," Jessica reminded her when Sharon finally took a breath, leaving Jessica with a chance to speak.

"I forgot them."

"Don't pick it out on me if you forgot the keys. The painkillers are in the bathroom for the hangover. I've ice-pops in the freezer." Jessica pointed as she brushed past.

"Oh, you sure know how to spoil a girl." Sharon's eyes lit up. "And what's wrong with you? You're as pale as a ghost."

"Bad dream," Jessica answered honestly, walking away before Sharon could ask her anything else.

She finished making her bed when Sharon strolled in, an orange flavoured ice-pop swinging from her dehydrated mouth.

"God bless the ice-pop, and may they never run out of ice to make them," Sharon hailed as she threw herself on the bed. The one Jessica just made.

"Hello. I've just made the bed," she stated, waving her hands in question.

"Thanks." Sharon shrugged, rolling over and switching on the small television with the remote.

"Not for you, you shithead," Jessica muttered as she sat next to her friend, both resting their heads in their hands and swinging their legs behind them.

"What time is he picking you up?" Sharon mumbled, the ice-pop stuffed in her mouth.

"Six."

Sharon almost choked.

"Are you okay?"

"Six o'clock?" Sharon squeezed from her lips.

"Uh-huh."

"Jess, it's ten minutes past one. Start getting ready. Now!" Sharon demanded. Her worried face made her nose wrinkle.

"Sharon, I have five hours to get dressed. Calm down."

"No, you have four hours and fifty minutes. Big difference." Sharon nodded frantically, biting down on the tangy orange ice as she jumped from the bed.

"There's ten minutes in the difference. And I'm not you. It doesn't take me hours to get ready."

"Well, it should. You are going to the most talked about party of the year with Jake. You want to impress him, so his mouth hits the floor. Miss, you should have been getting ready since this morning."

Jessica could see her mouth moving, but she couldn't hear any of the words. It was like she had a switch in her brain to put her on mute. She thought herself how to do it over the years. Being friends with Sharon all your life can take its toll.

She was pretty sure they did it to each other.

"Get up," Sharon bellowed, dragging Jessica from the bed. "Go and wash. Come on. You have given me very little time to work with you."

"Work with me?" She croaked, sounding scared.

Sharon's claws were out, and she was about to feel every bit of them.

"Not that you need much, but it will calm me down if I know you're doing something."

"Okay. Fine. I'll have a shower if it makes you feel better. The last thing I want is you throwing a hissy fit. This apartment is too small for one of your tantrums," Jessica teased before she pondered into the bathroom to have a shower.

Four hours later, Jessica emerged from her bedroom and into the living room, where Sharon sat waiting for her. But just before leaving her bedroom, she granted herself one look in the full-length mirror. Her off-the-shoulder emerald green gown hugged her womanly curves and flowed down her body. The lace bodice embraced her breasts and A-line bottom flowed to the ground.

Sharon insisted on doing her makeup. Dark, smoky eyeshadow made her ocean blue eyes explode against the colours and it reflected her neutral lip gloss on her creamy skin. She straightened her dark auburn hair and pinned it up loosely so many messy pieces were falling in around her face.

"Here it goes," she breathed before making her way towards the living room. Her heels sounded like bombs against the wooden floor.

"Oh. My. God. He won't be able to keep it in his pants. You look beautiful." Sharon hugged her close. "But I think it's time for me to go because he will be here any minute."

"Thanks for everything. You may be a pain in the ass sometimes, but you are always there for me."

"You're my favourite pain in the ass, too. I'm only giving back for everything you have done for me." Sharon winked before she left.

Now that Jessica was by herself, the silence consumed her, and the butterflies and nervousness kicked in again. She saw Jake every day, but it didn't stop her mouth from going dry when she pictured his reaction to seeing her.

Rummaging through her bag to find her ringing phone, her nerves upped their power over her, seeing Jake's name pop up on the screen.

"Hi," she answered.

"Hello, gorgeous. I'm outside the building. I'll be up in a minute."

"Stay downstairs. Wait in the lobby."

"If you insist."

The buzz of the lobby hummed in the background. This was her Julia Roberts in *Pretty Woman* moment. Only she wasn't a prostitute.

The elevator ride on the way down felt like the longest ever. She wanted to see his face already.

As the doors opened to the warm, busy lobby, she stepped out and smiled as she watched him standing by the door. He was even more handsome in a black tuxedo. His hands in his pocket, standing tall, calm and drop-dead gorgeous, staring out onto the street through the glass door. His physique stood unmoving and strong, and the sun shining on him only enhanced his sallow skin and dark eyes.

He was oblivious to the stares of other women on their comings and goings through the lobby. It was a natural reaction. Jessica didn't blame them. She wasn't blind. Even she could appreciate his sex appeal. His broad shoulders had the strength to pick you up and do as he pleased.

With that thought and the urge to extinguish the sudden heat rushing to her core, she finally found the courage to put one foot in front of the other. Halting when she finally reached him, she stayed silent for a moment, waiting for him to say something. He didn't. He spun around, sensing her as she always sensed him, and he simply stared.

And stared.

Still staring.

"Why are you looking at me like that?" she questioned, the words leaving her mouth slowly in fear he might say something she didn't want to hear.

Did she have lipstick on her teeth?

Still, he didn't speak. Instead, he made her heart leap with a passionate kiss.

"Jesus, Jess, you're stunning," he whispered after she took a second for a deep breath, his mouth hovering close to her ear. His breath caused a tingle across her neck.

"You don't look so bad yourself."

All he did was smile, his gaze never faltering from hers. No cocky remark about how he already knew how gorgeous he was.

"Could you stop looking at me now?" She laughed nervously, feeling suddenly self-conscious.

"I can't," he confessed, making her heart do double flips in her chest. She looked away, trying to hide the embarrassment flushing through her cheeks.

Eventually, he placed his hand on her lower back, ushering her towards the door. Her eyes widened as they stepped outside where a limo was waiting.

"A limo? Why am I not surprised?"

"Yes," he dragged out, sounding as if he were unsure about how to answer.

"We could have used your car. God knows it's fancy enough."

"Jess, it's the biggest event of the year. We weren't about to show up in anything less than a limo. Now shut up and get in. It's cold out here in case you haven't noticed." Jake smiled softly, rubbing her cheek with his thumb, and guiding her towards the limo.

As they pulled away from her building, she felt Jake's eyes on her again. She turned to face him and breathed a laugh as his eyes met hers.

"Seriously, please stop staring at me," she begged, feeling her cheeks blush once again. He must have noticed, because he placed his fingers along her jawline, muttering something incoherent.

"You're too damn beautiful for your own good. Do you know that?" He shrugged, dropping his hand.

"Close your eyes," she blurted.

"What?"

"I want you to stop staring at me, so I need to find a way to stop you. Just close your eyes."

After a long moment, he gave in and shut his eyes. She licked her lips and leaned closer to him, slowly pressing her mouth against his, ravishing in the quiet moan he let out as she did so. She could feel his hand clasping in around hers. He gripped it tightly and continued kissing her as if it were the last kiss they would ever share.

She raised her leg, half straddling him and feeling a rush as the suit material rubbed against her inner thigh.

Instinctively, his hand clasped around the bare flesh and pulled her closer. With their breathing frantic and erratic, her rational mind pulled away. If she wanted to look half decent on his arm, she needed to stop. Having their way with each other in the limo would only prove counterproductive.

They both stopped when the limo did. Gasping for air, they stared at each other.

"You ruined my lipstick."

"You don't need that stuff, anyway."

He got out when the door opened and stood, gesturing his hand to help her.

Outside, the venue was decorated with bright white lights, and other shivering couples made their way up the mountain of steps into the heated ballroom. Jessica linked her arm in Jake's, and he led her inside, where the large room was beautifully embellished in black and gold. Servers were rushing around with trays, while people danced to the music of the jazz band, and others mingled.

"I think every man in the room just noticed you walk in here, Jess. They can't stop looking at you."

"It doesn't make a difference to me." She bit down on her glossed lip.

"Why?"

"Because you're looking at me."

She watched as his lips curved up into a smug smile.

"And I will always be looking at you." He kissed the top of her head, and she swallowed hard as she stared up at him.

But the feeling Jessica experienced in her dream this morning suddenly punched her in the gut.

Her heart began to race and pound behind her ears. The rush of blood made her queasy. She should have already known why.

There she was. Just as clear as she was in her dream.

Katie was gliding towards them, in all her unmistakable beauty.

FIFTEEN

When you try to act calm and try not to give anything away, you always make it ten times worse. Or so Jessica learned when Jake looked at her as if she had multiple heads.

"Jess, are you okay?"

Slowly, she turned from the golden-haired goddess making her way towards them.

"Looks like we have company," she breathed, looking away from him.

She wanted to hide her jealousy. She could never compare to Katie. Jake had loved her with all his heart. She was his first love, and for all Jessica knew, he could very well still love her.

"What are you talking about?" His eyes narrowed, making his eyebrows furrow into a deep, mysterious look.

Why did that man have to turn her on in the most awkward of places? He didn't mean to, but it showed her how deeply attracted she was to him.

She decided she needed to answer him and lose all hope of him looking at her for the rest of the night. Once he saw Katie, he was going to melt. So, one last time, she let his eyes bore through her, seizing her closer and drinking her in.

But he didn't let go when she tried to back away from his touch. He reached in and kissed her so passionately he stole the breath from her lungs. He turned his body a little, so he was completely flush with against her. His toned torso pressed against her as he took her face in his hands and kissed her as he had never kissed her before. She shivered as his fingers danced down her neck and across her collarbone. This kiss was different. Weighted in passion. But his movements were soft, as if he didn't want to break her. He could have taken her home right there and then, and she wouldn't have complained.

She moaned against his lips when he pulled away. Her breathing slowing down as her heartbeat raced inside her chest.

"I couldn't resist. You were staring up at me, looking so damn helpless." He rubbed his fingers along her cheekbone.

"Jake," she whispered. She hadn't looked, but Katie must have been very close by now. "Katie—"

"Jake, how are you?"

She watched as he turned his head to the familiar voice, but his expression never faltered from that sexy, irresistible smile he plastered on his face. It was the smile Jessica happily fell for many times before.

"Katie. Long-time, no see," he said, reaching out to kiss the olive skin on her cheek.

She seemed taken aback.

"You look lovely. As always," he added, turning back to Jessica to grace her with a caring wink. She didn't know what he did, but she didn't seem so worried about Katie anymore. He made her feel like she was the only woman in the room.

"And Jessica." Katie turned to look at her without question.

"Katie, how have you been?" Jessica edged a simple smile and tried to sound as nice as she could. Nicer than she felt, at least.

"Good. I never realized you and Jake were together. I never saw that one coming." She waved a long fingernail between them both. The hint of sarcasm in her tone didn't go unnoticed.

"Ah, we're…" Jessica hesitated, unsure of how to answer.

What were they?

Jake wrapped a supportive arm around her waist and squeezed gently. "We're doing really well," Jake backed in, and she sighed with sheer relief.

But wait, did he just agree they were together?

Katie had seen him with his tongue back her throat, which must have been his reasoning.

"And you always were a poor liar, Katie." He shook his head, smiling to himself.

Her eyes widened. There were a thousand silent words spoken

between them.

"Never saw it coming?" he repeated, chuckling deeply under his breath. She made a mental note to ask him what he meant about that.

"Have a lovely evening, Katie." Jake reached in once again to kiss her cheek. "I think your fiancé is on his way over here."

As they walked away, Jessica looked back at a dumbstruck Katie, biting on her red-painted lip.

"Have a seat." Jake pulled out a chair at a large round table for her to sit.

They were the only people sitting. Everyone else was walking around, getting into conversations with other business colleagues. The hall was full of people in glamorous gowns and tuxedos. The warm-coloured lights reflected down on the band and orchestra. Jessica was sure with one or two more champagnes, those women with the glamorous gowns would make their mark on the dance floor.

"Do you miss her?" she finally asked, breaking his intense gaze by looking away.

He exhaled loudly, gushing his surprise. "Wasn't expecting that."

"Do you?"

"No," he answered, and from the firmness of his voice, she believed him.

She noticed he didn't look at Katie the way he used to when they were in love. As much as Jessica used to despise Jake, she always admired the way he looked at Katie, the way he protected her.

"If you asked me that question last year, my answer may have been different. I don't know what it is, but I felt nothing." And he meant it. She could see it in his eyes.

"I see why you loved her, though." Jessica looked over to where Katie was standing. Her shimmering gold dress fell loosely from under her breast and her blonde, bob-cut hair fell to just above her shoulders, exposing her bare back. "She is stunning."

"You have no idea, do you? You have no idea how amazingly beautiful you are. There's no comparison, Jess. Every woman in this room is going to hate you because they want to be you. Every man in this room is going to hate me because I'm with you."

He curled his fingers under her chin, tilting her face so she was looking at him, then he placed a gentle kiss on her lips. She was glad she wore blush on her cheeks because they were burning like a fire.

"You're going to have to stop that."

"I can't." He winked, probably at the flushed expression on her face.

She was blushing because of this man. She was turning into a teenage girl. She needed saving from his charm, but the only person who could save her was herself.

Guess what?

She was too lazy to save herself. It was too much effort to resist him anymore.

But she needed to, didn't she? Wasn't the whole reason she was trying to stay away from him in the beginning was because she didn't want to get hurt?

But what if she didn't have lots of time left to live her life? Was she better to live it the best way she knew how?

She didn't know, but right now, Jake made her feel things she never felt before, and she wouldn't throw that away. Not tonight, anyway.

Maybe tomorrow.

"You okay there, Jess?" Jake tilted his head.

"Sorry. I was in one of my trances."

"Uh-huh." He raised an eyebrow in suspicion. "By the way." His expression soon changed to one of suspense, and his lips curved up into a cheeky grin. "Don't be mad, but look at what I got."

Her jaw dropped as he pulled out a small square card from his inside pocket.

"You got us a room?" she questioned.

"Well, you know. Going back to one of our places is too far. I don't think I can wait that long."

"You could have told me. I don't have any clothes."

"Baby, where we are going, you don't need clothes."

"I have to choose my words wisely with you. Now give me that." She grabbed the key from his hand, laughing at the distraught look on his face. "Believe me, it's safer if I keep it in my bag. You have a habit of losing things."

As she looked over his shoulder, Jessica saw another familiar face gliding towards her. It was Mr. Johnson's wife, Nora.

"Is that our Jessica?" Nora squealed, reaching out her arms.

Immediately, Jessica rose from her chair and embraced the well-rounded woman. Her chestnut brown hair was pinned back neatly, and her pale eyes glistened. As her smile widened, her small wrinkles bore deeper into her skin.

"Hi Nora," Jessica managed as she hugged her closer.

"You look absolutely stunning, honey."

"Thank you," Jessica said, feeling the heat from Jake's body on her back.

"Jake, my dear, there you are." Nora hugged and kissed him on the cheek. "You look very handsome. You know how to pick them, love." She smiled at Jessica.

"You look wonderful, Nora." Jake motioned with his hand, using his charming ways. It came to him like second nature. He made this sixty-year-old woman blush like a girl.

"I'm going to get a drink."

Jessica shivered, feeling Jake's breath on her neck, smiling as he whispered in his ear, "Vodka and orange juice? Or do you still drink that stuff, because I can't remember it doing you any good when you were twenty-one?"

"White wine, please."

Jessica grimaced at the blurred memories of her 21st birthday. She remembered some tables and a pole, and she danced on and around all of them.

"And a white wine for you too?" He smiled at Nora, who willingly accepted his offer.

That night, after the meal, the conversation at the table flowed just as well as the alcohol did. Jessica knew she couldn't risk getting drunk, not with the medication she was taking. And she could feel a headache coming on, pounding at her temple.

"I'll be back in a minute," she promised Jake as she left to use the restroom.

Once she got inside, she opened her small bag and grabbed the tube of pills. She tried her best to swallow it without water. It was a struggle, but she managed it. At least this time she wouldn't have Jake fussing over her because she fainted into his arms.

How cliche?

She quickly fixed her makeup, applied some lipstick, and made her way towards the main hall once again. But not everything was the same as when she left.

She thought her heart tore into shreds as her feet brought her nearer to the table. Katie was wrapped in Jake's arms on the dance floor. Both of their feet were moving in unison.

It's just a dance. Calm down. Get a grip on yourself, Jessica reminded herself, taking a deep breath.

The song stopped as Jessica began moving again, and they all reached the table at the same time. Katie offered herself to Jessica's seat. But what she saw next made her want to run back to the toilet and throw her heart up. She watched as Katie's perfectly manicured fingers travelled up and down Jake's leg and she had no sign of stopping. He caught her hand and pushed her away. It gave Jessica some consolation, but it didn't stop the bitterness from boiling.

"We were going out for over ten years."

Jessica caught the conversation Katie was having with the entire table as she sat down on the vacant chair on the other side of Jake.

She felt uncomfortable even being there.

"You okay?" Jake finally asked after a few moments. "You're as pale as a ghost, sweetheart."

He was probably right. She could still feel the pounding at her temples, but she knew the medication would set in soon.

"I'm fine," she said weakly, knowing he might not have heard her because of the music.

"And we were engaged for two years," Katie went on, making Jessica's gaze travel to her.

Everyone seemed intrigued to meet Jake's ex-fiancé.

Pity Jessica wasn't so eager to hear about it.

"Isn't that lovely? I can't believe you two were going out since school," a young woman replied. She was sitting at the table with Jessica all night, but she still hadn't a clue who she was.

"Yes. Yes, it was," Katie slurred, and for the first time, Jessica noticed the glossiness in her eyes and the way she swayed in her seat.

She was drunk.

Very drunk.

The last time Jessica remembered Katie drunk was the night she did a striptease outside a nightclub. Did that girl not learn to take it slow?

"Jake won't love anybody else the way he loved me," Katie stated, staring up at him. Jake's face formed into a state of rage.

"I think that's enough," he told her, a secret warning hidden in his words.

"But it's true. Nobody will be good enough for you. You won't find another like me. I think you should just take me back." She fell onto his shoulder and the entire table erupted into laughter.

"I need a minute," Jessica told him once again, shooting up from her seat like it was on fire.

She couldn't listen to it. She knew she wasn't good enough for Jake, but she didn't need it rubbed in her face.

For too long, Rob had told her she wasn't worth anything, and she wasn't good enough for anyone. A part of her had tried for so long to tell herself it wasn't true. Another part couldn't help but believe it.

Her shaking hands reached into her bag, her fingers beating lipstick and eyeshadows out of her way.

"It's a tiny bag. How hard can it be to find a key card?" Through gritted teeth, she mumbled, cursing to herself.

Even when she found it, she fumbled, fighting back tears of frustration.

Then she found herself having to suppress a scream when a warm hand covered hers.

"Let me get it," Jake offered, opening the heavy door into the suite.

"Christ, do you always sneak up on people?" she spat, feeling her pulse go out of control.

He merely offered a soft as he gestured for her to go inside. She walked in, feeling the warmth of the modern room. Black, white and red seemed to be the reoccurring theme throughout the far too large space, where a huge four-poster bed stood in the center.

The room felt too big. It wasn't small enough to contain the bubbling of emotions threatening to rupture.

"I'm sorry about that," he whispered, closing the door behind him.

Tears stung her eyes, and she hated it. She didn't want to cry over this man.

"It's not your fault." Her voice sounded weak and vulnerable as she placed her bag on the table.

"Look at me, Jess."

She closed her lids, letting the silence of the room cradle her. She didn't want to look at him and feel things because she didn't even know what she felt anymore.

"Jess," he repeated, his voice agitated and pleading.

"What Jake?" she snapped, turning around to face him.

Instantly, she shook her head, trying her best to let the bad thoughts escape. She didn't want to let her tears fall. She didn't want to let him see her cry.

"What the hell is wrong with you?"

"I don't know," she answered honestly. She hadn't the slightest clue what was wrong with her. Maybe she was mad at herself. Maybe it was the jealousy she had no right to feel.

"Are you going to figure it out soon?" His voice was rising in pitch, and she knew he was getting annoyed with her.

"Maybe. Are you going to stop confusing me anytime soon?"

"What do you mean?"

"I don't know what you want from me, Jake." She bit down on her full bottom lip. She needed to think. "Sometimes, I think you're great. But then, I can't help but wonder, all those amazing things you say, are they just to get me into bed?" She felt the tears welling up in her eyes, threatening to spill over.

"Do you honestly think I do all of that just to get you into bed? Don't be so stupid."

"I'm not being stupid. I'm preparing myself because, let's face it, you're not exactly the virgin of the year. I thought I could do this. I thought I could get through this in one piece, but we just end up at square one all the time."

"You're completely blind."

He was mad now. Really mad. She could hear the flaming anger erupting from his lips.

"You know what? Forget about it," she fought, storming past him in a rage. She had enough.

But she should have known, even if she had enough, he didn't, and he caught her wrist, swinging her around to face him.

"I'm fighting for you. It's you I've been fighting for all along."

Her eyes widened in shock, and a single tear trailed down her cheek.

"Can't you see that? Even Katie could see it. She had an affair because of me."

"Jake, don't blame—"

"No, it's true. And I don't blame her. I should probably thank her." He shrugged, loosening his grip.

"We weren't always the happy couple people saw. We fought over the simplest of things. Mainly you."

Her breath caught in her throat.

What was he talking about? What had she to do with their relationship?

"To her, you were a simple thing. To me, you were something totally different. I don't even know if you remember this, or even care, but I used to call you every night when you were with Rob. I wanted to make sure you were doing okay. I knew what he was like, but you wouldn't let me get involved because you said you loved him. And it killed me. It killed me to hear you say you loved somebody else. And I don't even know why, because I thought we hated each other. Then when I saw the bruises, and all I wanted to do was protect you. Katie wasn't stupid. She could see it. She couldn't say a bad word about you, and I snapped."

She gasped, her chest rising and falling frantically.

"Jake," she begged as the tears flowed freely from her eyes.

"No. You need to listen. We fought in that relationship until I realized I was fighting my way out of it. I was fighting for you. And I have been stupid enough to not want to see it until the last couple of months." He moved his hands to her face and stroked her tears with his thumb. "What if my mother was right, Jess? What if you are the one that has been worth fighting for all along?" He paused for a moment, searching her face for something. "Christ Jess, I've fallen in love with you."

She looked up into his big brown eyes, unable to find the words to speak. Not the right ones.

He admitted everything she wanted to hear. But he also confirmed everything she dreaded hearing.

"So even if you don't believe me, I won't give up fighting until you do. Just promise you'll still be here."

God, she hated irony.

"I'm not very good at keeping promises," she cried.

"You will if I hold on tightly enough."

Then he leaned in and crushed her with his kiss, backing her up against the door where his body pressed against hers.

And at that moment, she knew she had lost it.

No, not her mind.

Her heart.

SIXTEEN

Jessica blinked at the heavy fog in her eyes and rubbed away the sleep while she embraced the warmth she was wrapped in. Her throat was dry, her lips swollen, and her hair matted against the pillow, but she didn't care. It didn't stop the joy of butterflies swirling around inside.

She hadn't opened her eyes yet, but she knew he was there. She knew his arms were surrounding her as if he were trying to protect her from something.

A soft smile gathered on her kissed-out lips as she pondered every word Jake said to her the night before.

She was the one he was fighting for. The wild look in his eyes scared her but brought a heat to her body like she never knew possible.

Last night, when he told her, relief and fear hit at once.

Relief he felt the same way she did, and fear, because she was doing exactly what she told herself she wouldn't. She was going to hurt him, and she had the power to stop it. But she couldn't let him go. It just took her years to realize it. She couldn't tell him either. It gave her chills to even think of sitting him down and watching the look on his face as she told him she was fighting cancer. Cancer that could never give him children. And he wanted them so badly.

Shaking the uneasy thought from her head, she finally found the strength to open her eyes. When she did, she was greeted by the relaxed face and gentle breathing of Jake's body. He looked so peaceful; so happy.

He was there through everything. She never thanked him for that.

The night before, he didn't think she remembered when he used to call her, not just after Rob, but when she was in that relationship.

She remembered.

Jessica remembered every single conversation she had with him, and she didn't realize why until last night. It was because she loved the man lying beside her; the man she hugged so close, she never wanted to let go. She was always too scared to admit it to herself because the last time she let her guard down and loved somebody, she got hurt. They took her heart from her chest and stomped on it like a piece of dirt stuck to the ground.

She allowed her fingers over Jake's eyes and brushed them along his lips, remembering how he put shivers through her body at the slightest glance.

Quickly, she pulled her hand away, feeling a heavy breath sweep across her face, and his eyes fluttered to life.

"Sorry," Jessica whispered against his chest, feeling guilty for waking him.

When his eyes opened to the dim light of the room, he looked down at her, his relaxed yet dark features making her feel meek beneath him. He was giving her *that* look. She knew it was coming. This man was about to make her his own. She was the only one he wanted right then, and she fed on it. In fact, she needed it.

So, it was no surprise when his lips landed on hers. She trembled under his touch and the feel of his tongue grazing her bottom lip, exploring her mouth. As he did, he pulled her closer to his heated, muscular body, his fingers dancing up and down her squirming figure.

"Don't be sorry," he said, pulling back for air, still not letting go of the secure grip around her body.

For a long moment, he just stared at her in silence, making the blood rush to her cheeks with embarrassment. He laughed under his breath and placed his fingers under her chin to lift her face back to meet his eyes.

"You're adorable when you do that." He kissed her gently.

"Stop doing it," Jessica demanded, slapping him playfully on the arm.

"You're too damn beautiful. I can't help it."

"What time is it?" she asked, directing the subject away from herself.

As he leaned over to look at his watch on the locker, she took the chance to appreciate his toned torso and the way his muscles stretched.

"It's almost time for us to get up." He yawned, turning back to look at her. She cuddled closer, not wanting to get up. She never wanted to leave that very spot.

"I know, baby." He rubbed his hand along her back. "Me neither," he continued, as if he could read her thoughts.

As she lay there in his arms, she noticed some things scattered along the floor. It was her dress and underwear, leaving a trail across the large hotel room. Her beautiful dress was a ball of wrinkles in the corner.

"I wish you'd have told me we were staying the night. I would've brought some fresh clothes." She tilted her head to stare up and him. "Now I have to do the walk of shame."

"It must have slipped my mind last night, but I have everything in check. There's a bag in the wardrobe with everything you could need in it."

"But how?"

"Sharon," he answered quickly. "I called her last week and asked her to do me a favour. I assume she is about the only one who knows about us."

"You mean she knew about this before I did?"

"She did."

"What made you so confident I was going to stay?"

"I wasn't going to take no for an answer."

She inhaled sharply as he rolled her over, pinning her hands to the pillow above her head, and hovered over her.

"Jake!" she shrieked.

"Hush," he growled, coming closer to her face. This man was growling at her like a beast. She whimpered quietly as he left a map of kisses down her neck, across her jawline, over her collarbone, studying the reactions of her body like a book; a book he seemed engrossed in, yet not once removing the grip he had on her hands over her head. Instead, he intertwined his fingers with hers, holding them tight, keeping her there so he could do what he liked. He was keeping her secure, and she loved it. Another trail of kisses along her skin, and then he blew cold air over the moisture his lips had left, smiling with satisfaction at her soft pleas. He looked at her then, making her feel he could see into her for miles.

Unable to stop herself, Jessica slowly lifted her head and met his lips with a soft passionate kiss, embracing the way he let one of his hands glide over her soft, bare skin. The other hand he kept over her head. Her breath was coming in heavy pants as his hands travelled over her black satin underwear.

"You've got to be fucking with me." She gritted her teeth, her ears protesting against her buzzing phone.

Jake sighed against her lips and pulled away before kissing her one last time.

"You better get that." He nodded towards the phone.

She mentally cursed the person on the other end of the line before she tapped to answer, not bothering to even check the name.

"Hello?" she sighed, sitting up, throwing her long legs over the edge of the bed.

"Jessica?" A familiar voice wondered.

"Yes," she said slowly, trying to recognize who the voice belonged to.

"Jessica, this is Doctor Harris."

Frantically, she placed her hand over the mouthpiece of the phone and turned to Jake.

"I'm going to take this in the bathroom. It's April. Men problems," she lied, hoping the smile on her face convinced him enough not to question her.

He shook his head and winked.

"Put this on." He grabbed his white shirt from the black carpeted floor and threw it at her.

She shrugged her arms into it.

"Sexy," he hissed as she pondered into the bathroom, closing the door behind her.

"Sorry about that, Doctor Harris," Jessica finally spoke. "Is there something wrong?" Her voice was almost a whisper. She didn't want Jake to get suspicious.

"Oh, no. I didn't mean to worry you. I'm calling to find out if you'd like to move your scan forward to tomorrow. We got a cancellation today, and I thought of you. I know you're a busy woman, and it will ease some worries to get it out of the way."

She plopped herself on the edge of the large bath and exhaled loudly, letting her pulse slow down.

"Tomorrow is good."

Was the man trying to give her a heart attack? Because she was well on her way to one.

"Perfect. I will see you at two."

"See you then." She sounded breathless as she said goodbye.

She tried her best to calm her heartbeat, but it wouldn't obey. Slowly, she stood, clinging to the sink for support as the bathroom spun around her. The familiar beads of sweat stuck to her skin and her pulse quickened again. This episode came on too fast.

When she closed her eyes, she took three deep breaths and swallowed the lump forming in her throat. Thankfully, when she opened them again, the only thing left was the clamminess on her skin.

She splashed some cold water on her face before she made her way back into the room, where Jake was pulling a grey sweater over his head. Once his face was visible, she smiled at him for a moment before strolling towards him, standing on her tiptoes to kiss him.

"Everything good with April?"

"Everything is fine," she simply said, removing the bag Sharon packed for her.

She didn't want to look at him when she lied.

Throwing the bag on the bed, she opened it to see her blue faded jeans and a white fitted blouse folded neatly inside. She made a mental note to kiss Sharon when she saw her. She pulled off his shirt, exposing her bare shoulders.

"Here." She threw it at him, making him jump.

"It looked better on you." He shrugged, looking disappointed she had taken it off.

She dressed and tied her hair back loosely.

"You know, we will probably have to tell people about us at work," Jake announced as they made their way into the elevator.

"You mean there is an *us*?" she teased, nudging him as the steel doors closed.

"We work well together. It can't be that hard." He grazed his fingers over her cheekbone.

They were going to do this. She was totally and utterly insane.

What if he genuinely loved her? She was dying, and she couldn't bear the thought of telling him. She couldn't.

"We'll see," Jessica finally whispered.

Before he could react, the large steel doors opened onto the luxurious lobby they had entered the night before. The daylight shone on the marble tiles and reflected throughout the large space. Sofas and chairs spread out neatly, and the friendly faces of the receptionists beamed behind the counter.

As they stepped out, Jessica could feel her mouth water again.

"For Christ's sake," she muttered under her breath. "Jake, will you take a seat for a moment? I need a minute."

"No problem. I'll checkout."

She quickened her speed the more her throat filled with a lump. Her head pounded against her temples, and her vision became blurred.

"Not now. Not now."

She reached the cubicle in time. The pressure in her stomach became too much, and she threw up, feeling her body become weak and lifeless. Standing and wiping her mouth, she supported herself against the wall and waited for her erratic pulse to calm.

Giving herself another long moment, she slipped out of the small cubicle.

And oh, how she wished she had stayed inside when she was greeted by the red-painted lips and golden hair of Katie, staring at her through the mirror as she applied mascara to her short eyelashes.

"Feeling sick, Jessica?" Katie asked coolly, zooming closer to the mirror to concentrate on her makeup.

Jessica bit down on her now pale bottom lip before she made her way to the sink.

"Something I ate."

She twisted the tap, rubbed some soap onto her hands, and washed them. The last thing she wanted was a heart-to-heart chat.

"You and Jake seem pretty close." Katie turned to her, leaning her hip against the counter. "Something I should know about?"

"I don't think it's any of your business," Jessica stated calmly. This was the wrong day for Katie to get on her nerves. Her head ached and her stomach was doing somersaults. "What Jake and I do is between nobody but us."

"So, you admit you are doing something?"

"Katie, I don't want to have this conversation with you right now. You and Jake are over. You have been for a while. He moved on and you are engaged, so I assume that you have moved on, too. Look, I know you two will always have something. You were together for so long and engaged to be married, but some things just don't work out."

She gulped back the pain. The throbbing in her head was getting worse and a confrontation with Katie wasn't helping.

"You could never love him like I love him. He is passing time with you."

"What? Until he comes crawling back to you? You slept with another man," Jessica snapped. "You hurt him, Katie. But you don't have him wrapped around your little finger anymore."

Jessica's gaze on her narrowed as she cackled.

"You honestly think he cared about me? Do you think I was the one who had him wrapped around my finger? If you said jump, he asked how high."

For the first time, Jessica experienced a pang of sympathy for the golden-haired beauty standing in front of her.

"That doesn't mean he didn't care about you. He loved you."

"But you won in the end. Having an abusive boyfriend really gave you the upper hand," Katie spat, her lip trembling with anger.

"I don't have to explain myself to you. Jake and I have known each other for a long time. He was trying to protect me." Jessica took a deep breath before speaking again. "I wouldn't expect you to understand. Jake treated you like a queen and you pushed him away. This isn't about winning, but if you asked me, you gave him away. You didn't fight for him. Now, if you don't mind, I need to leave."

She stormed out of the bathroom, adrenaline pumping through her veins. The clamminess on her skin made her blood seem cold as the air met her skin.

"Sweetheart?" He must have noticed the bewildered look on her face. "Jess, what's wrong?" He pressed his hands against her face.

Focus.

That's what she needed to do. She needed to focus on Jake.

"I'm fine."

"Sit down." He pushed her gently onto the leather sofa. "You're not fine."

"I'm cold."

"Jess?"

"I'm okay, honestly. Will you bring me home?" she pleaded, blocking the sun from her eyes with her hand.

"You need a doctor."

"No doctor. Just bring me home. It's a headache."

He opened his mouth to argue with her, but she hushed him with her finger.

"Just take me home," she begged as she rested her head on his shoulder, shielding her eyes from the sun.

"Okay."

Twenty minutes later, they were both sitting in a taxi on their way to Jessica's apartment. As she dozed off in his arms, his phone rang, but she didn't have the energy to dwell on his conversation.

When her eyes opened again, she was lying on her sofa with a large blanket over her body.

"Did you carry me all the way up here?" Jessica asked, noticing Jake sitting at the other end of the sofa, watching the muted television, his hands relaxed on her legs.

"You demanded to walk. You slapped me a few times when I even tried to help you."

"Sorry."

"You need to go to a doctor."

Jake stood only to crouch down beside her, removing the strands of hair from her face and kissing her softly on the forehead. Unfortunately, this wasn't a pain he could kiss better.

"Jess?"

"Yes?"

"Who was on the phone earlier? In the hotel room?"

Her gaze narrowed as she stared at him.

"April," she lied.

"Yeah, that's the thing." He exhaled deeply. "April called me in the taxi. We got talking, and she hasn't spoken to you since yesterday. Who was on the phone, Jess?"

Her eyes widened in shock. How the hell was she supposed to get herself out of this one?

She sat there for a long moment, taking in deep breaths, trying not only to soothe the pounding at her temples but to buy herself more time. Jake was searching her face, as if he knew exactly what she was trying to do. The pain grew, and her mouth watered as nausea sailed through her body. Her palms gripped the cushions of the couch, and she wished she could melt into it. How was she going to tell him?

She couldn't. She couldn't hurt him. Not like this.

She opened her mouth to speak just as her phone buzzed on the coffee table. She looked back and forth between her phone and Jake's scrutinizing stare.

She leaned over, reaching out for it before he had a chance to stop her.

She looked at the numbers flashing, and a familiar tingle gnawed at her back. No name, just numbers.

"Aren't you going to answer that?" Jake asked anxiously.

She looked up at him before obeying.

"Hello?" she managed, her head aching as if it were a strain for her to speak.

"Jessica? Is that you?"

The colour drained from her cheeks, her blood pooling at her feet. She wasn't going mad. Those numbers gleaming at her just moments ago were all too familiar indeed.

As she stretched her legs over the sofa to stand, Jake's firm grip stopped her. "You're not going anywhere. I need to know what the hell is going on."

It suddenly felt like somebody had reached their hand through her throat and into her chest.

She looked at Jake once more, pleading with him before she even opened her mouth to say a word.

He was going to go insane. She knew it.

"Jessica?" the deep, worried voice interrupted. "Are you there?

"I'm here." She swallowed. "What do you want, Rob?" she asked, shifting as Jake's body tensed, his tight jaw flexing under strain. She looked away, not daring to look him straight in the eye.

"I'm sorry, but you're the only person who can help," Rob stuttered over his words. He sounded upset.

"What's wrong?"

"It's my sister." His voice broke.

"What's happened?"

"The day we met, I told you she had a baby boy, right?"

"Yes."

Where was he going with this?

"Afterwards, she got depressed. It was bad. She couldn't even look at the poor kid. The doctor told her it was postnatal depression, and with the help of medication, she would get better. It didn't help. Last week, her husband walked in after she had stuffed a tonne of pills into her mouth. She overdosed. They pumped her out or some shit like that. Physically, she's fine again, but mentally, she's not my sister anymore. She won't talk to anyone," he continued. "I know I can never excuse what I did to you, and I have no right to ask you for help, but she loved you. You were like a sister to her."

Before he could go on, Jessica cut him off. "I'll be there as soon as I can."

"Thank you," he whispered.

"Just remember, I'm not doing this for you."

"Of course, but thanks anyway," was the last thing she heard him say before she hung up.

Fiercely jumping as Jake grabbed the phone from her hand. It made a loud thud as he dropped it on the coffee table. His dark eyes were blazing, his breathing coming faster by the second.

"What the fuck is going on? Why is Rob calling you?" he shouted, demanding to know the answer to each of his questions.

"I'm not in the mood for this." Jessica shook her head as she kicked the heavy blanket from over her body and stood, making her way to the sink for a glass of water.

"I'm sorry. Would you like me to come at another time?" Jake asked sarcastically as she swayed, having to grab onto the kitchen counter for support.

Slowly, she turned to look at him. His eyes softened a little at the sight of her, so vulnerable and in pain, but he was still angry. She could tell by the fire blazing in his eyes.

"Was it him on the phone earlier?" he finally questioned, searching her face for a hint she was lying.

This was getting worse by the minute. It would have been easier to tell him it was the doctor who had called at the hotel, but he wouldn't believe her. Not now. Not when Rob just called.

She reached out to him. "Jake."

"Don't deny it."

"Nothing is going on, Jake," she defended.

He smiled coldly. "I never said there was."

"No, but you're thinking it."

"You have no idea what I'm thinking," he spat.

She scrubbed her fingers over her eyelids and took a deep breath.

"Look," she finally said, feeling the tears sting her eyes. She hurt him in her attempts to protect him. "His sister is sick. I need to see her. I'm not going anywhere near Rob. I swear."

"It's his sister. Why do you have to take care of her?"

He would never understand. It wasn't because he couldn't. It was because he didn't want to understand. Jake was stubborn. He always was.

"Because she trusts me, Jake. She needs someone to talk to, and I'm going to be there for her. And yes, maybe I'm crazy, but I have to go."

"What if Rob is making it up? Maybe he just wants to see you. Have you thought about that?"

Jessica looked him straight in the eyes. He pursed his lips into a hard line, and his jaw hardened. She smiled warmly, and he sighed.

"Your imagination is running wild."

He grunted loudly. "But yet, the secret phone call, and when he asks you to go over there, you go crawling."

She threw her arms out in frustration. "I am not crawling anywhere or to anyone."

Didn't that man realize he was killing her with just the look in his eyes?

Her eyes brimmed with tears as she took her steps toward him. She cupped his face, lazily brushing her thumb over his mouth, enjoying how his eyes closed, and how he trembled under her touch.

"You saw what he did to me. You were there."

His face flinched as he replayed the memories. But she needed him to remember.

"The physical pain he put me through was nothing compared to what went on in here." She grabbed his hand and pressed it against her chest, where her heart was racing frantically at the simple touch. "He hurt me, Jake. I'm not going back there again. I never will," she promised, biting down on her lip. "But I need to go."

He stepped away, and her arm fell to her side. Jake wasn't being reasonable, and she was already wasting time trying to tell him everything was going to be fine.

He gritted his teeth. "What's wrong with him, anyway?"

She looked at him, feeling confused for a moment. Had she not already told him it was his sister she was going to see?

"I'm going to see his sister."

"Give me a break, Jess. He called you twice today. What did he want earlier? A midday quickie? Was it the same usual time, usual place?"

Jessica felt like her heart was being squeezed by an iron fist. The tugging at her chest was unbearable, and a single tear trailed down her cheek like a brick falling from her face. She couldn't believe he said that to her. They always fought. It's what they did, but it was always playful, and she never gave it much notice. Now, it wasn't all that playful, she took notice, and it hurt like a slap in the face.

Promptly, she wiped away the moisture from her cheek and stood straight, doing her best to hide how much it was killing her to stand there and watch him look at her as if he despised her. His dark brown eyes were no longer soft and loving, but cold and distant.

"It's none of your business what the phone call was about earlier. You always were great for making assumptions," she said coldly, brushing past him to get her shoes.

"Hey, maybe I should pay a visit to see Katie."

She stopped dead in her tracks.

"That wouldn't be any of your business either, would it? I'm sure she wouldn't object."

Those words rang through with nothing but ice and venom.

Her eyes burned with the will to cry, but she couldn't. She felt weak and her knees buckled like jelly. Her blood had surely turned to water.

She laughed without any humour. "Maybe you should. I'm sure she would love that."

When she looked at him, his mouth slightly parted, his broad shoulders were tensed, and his eyes were wide. Maybe if she looked closely enough, she might even see regret.

Jessica turned, grabbed her brown boots, and stuck her feet into them.

One large stride toward her.

"Jess."

"Don't you dare." She stopped him, holding out her hand. "You were fighting for me?" She laughed hysterically. "That line was excellent. You always had a certain charm about you. Well, it worked. You got me into bed. Now go and tell Katie you are fighting for her. Maybe this time you'll speak the truth." She turned, grabbing her bag and keys. "You can see yourself out."

She shut the door, leaving a gobsmacked Jake and pieces of her shattered heart behind.

SEVENTEEN

Forty minutes later, and Jessica arrived outside Michelle's house. She made her way through the garden and knocked on the black-painted door of the red brick house.

"Lucas," Jessica exclaimed, smiling at Michelle's husband. She hadn't seen him since she broke up with Rob. He looked different. Dark circles painted on his smiling eyes, and his once boyish face looked tired and worn. He lost weight too, she noted. His black hair was peppered with grey, and stubble prickled his face.

"Oh, thank God. Thank you so much for coming," he said, guiding her into the house.

"It's no problem. I don't know if I can help, but I can try. Is she with the baby?" Jessica asked, forgetting why she was there. "I'm sorry." She felt like an idiot.

"That's okay." Lucas smiled, understanding written in his gentle smile. "She's in our room. She doesn't leave it."

She squeezed his arm supportively.

"Do you mind if I go up?"

"No, not at all. You know where to go."

As Jessica made her way upstairs, she suddenly realized that Rob wasn't even in the house. That made her blood boil even more. During her journey, her hurt turned to anger. She should have slapped Jake while she had the chance.

Shaking the thought from her head, she knocked gently on the bedroom door and turned the knob.

"Michelle," she called quietly.

She waited for a moment while her eyes adjusted to the dark room. The curtains were drawn. After a long, silent moment, there was a movement in the bed. Still standing at the door, she watched Michelle sit up. She remained there, not wanting to rush in.

"Who is it?" Michelle queried, her voice sounding tired.

"It's Jessica, M," she told her friend, using the nickname she always used.

Jessica cursed herself for ever losing contact.

The bedside lamp flicked on, filtering light throughout the large warm coloured bedroom.

"Jess?" Michelle edged from the bed, recognition spreading across her face. "Oh Jesus, Jess, what are you doing here?"

They both hugged each other tightly for a long moment and Jessica realized how much she missed her.

They both pulled away slowly, Michelle uncovering the purple bruise-like shadows below her eyes. From the lack of sleep, she guessed. Her sandy blonde hair was matted and tied up loosely. Her hazel eyes had lost their warmth and tenderness. She was awfully like Rob, only thinner, painfully so now. Even wrapped in her loose pyjamas, Jessica could tell her womanly curves had disappeared. She took a loose strand of Michelle's hair and placed it behind her ear.

"It looks like someone needs a good chat."

"Oh, Jess," Michelle cried onto her shoulder. "I don't know what is wrong with me."

"It's okay, sweetie." Jessica hugged her. "Come on, sit down." She guided her towards the bed. "I'm going to open the curtains. Is that okay with you?"

"Sure." She nodded, and Jessica slipped off her boots and sat next to her on the bed. "Rob called you, didn't he?"

"Yeah," Jessica answered honestly.

"I'm going to kill him. After everything he has put you through, he comes running to you for help."

Jessica's eyes narrowed. She never told his family.

"He told me," Michelle answered without any need for a question. "I wanted to know why you two broke up, and I kept on nagging until he gave in. I knew you wouldn't have left without some sort of reason. I should have known."

"Nobody knew, Michelle. And those who had suspicions towards the end didn't realize the severity."

"I'm so sorry I didn't keep in contact with you. I didn't know what to say."

"I understand. It's not your fault."

For twenty minutes, they spoke about general small news in each other's lives. No speaking of the dark past or turbulent present they both shared. Michelle's eyes glistened the whole time, her mind in battle with her body to keep the sobs from coming.

"You can talk to me. You know that, right?" Jessica offered.

"I know." She nodded, wiping away the pooling moisture. "That's why I'm glad you're here."

"Then talk to me."

Michelle took a long, deep breath before she began speaking. "I feel so isolated lately. After I had Ryan, everything was fine for the first week, but then I just kept on getting deeper into myself. I was crying for no reason and having unusual outbursts. But I thought it was natural. I was after giving birth. But after another few days, I constantly gave the baby to Lucas every chance I could. I couldn't bear to look at him, and I don't know why. I don't even feel like his mother. It feels like he belongs to someone else. And I can't talk to Lucas. He won't understand. And every time I want to talk to him, he gets mad. He thinks I don't care."

"Did he say that?"

"No," she answered. "But I know what he's thinking. It's not that I don't want to care for the baby. I do. I just think I'm going to mess up. And he is constantly crying. He never stops."

She inhaled the air surrounding her.

"Last week, I thought he would be better with me out of his life. It would make it easier for him. I grabbed all the painkillers I could find. God Jess, I'm a terrible mother," she sobbed.

"You're not," Jessica demanded. "Lots of mothers go through this, M. It's all right to be afraid and nobody is pushing you into this too fast. Take it slow," she assured. "I'll tell you what." Jessica stood. "You have a shower. That hair looks like birds are living in it," she laughed softly.

Michelle joined in, her laugh sounding brand new, like she hadn't used it in so long, and her cheeks blushed with embarrassment.

"Put on some fresh, comfortable clothes. When you are ready, I will be downstairs waiting for you."

"Then what?" Michelle questioned.

"We're taking Ryan for a walk. Just a short walk up and down the street. We can come back whenever you feel overwhelmed."

She looked scared. No, she looked petrified. Jessica thought she was going to crawl back under the covers and hide. But to her surprise, her friend stood and nodded.

"You're right. I have to start somewhere."

"Good girl." Jessica grinned as she watched Michelle stroll into her bathroom.

"Thanks, Jess." She smiled gratefully before she disappeared and closed the door behind her.

"How is she?" Lucas asked anxiously as she entered the living room. He was sitting on the cream sofa with the television volume on low. A bassinet was placed beside the sofa where the baby was sound asleep.

Sorry baby, she thought, *you are going to have to wake up soon because your mommy is getting her sanity back.*

"We're taking the baby for a walk."

He stared at her for a long moment, his eyes wide in his head. "You mean she's up and going out?"

"I don't know if she'll even go ahead with it yet, but she seemed hopeful. At least she's up and out of bed and having a shower. It's a start."

He stepped towards her before throwing his arms around her shoulders, hugging her until she could hardly breathe.

"You're a miracle worker," he said, pulling away from her. "When Rob called and said you were visiting, I agreed, but just because I was desperate. I don't mean that she didn't want to see you, but I didn't think she would accept help from anybody." He nodded in disbelief.

Jessica watched as tears fell from his eyes. The tears of a broken man, sleep deprived, and worried.

"She's going to get through this, Lucas. You both will," she assured him confidently. She knew how much Michelle wanted a baby. They tried for so long.

"I know he's sleeping, but would you mind if I held him?" Jessica asked, pointing towards the crib.

"Of course not."

Carefully, she pulled back the blanket, his tiny body smothered in warmth, and placed him comfortably in her arms, securing his head with her hand.

"Suits you," Lucas said, staring up at her from his chair.

"He's adorable," she whispered in awe.

He was so small he fitted perfectly in her arms. It hurt desperately to know she would never hold a baby she could call her own. She always wanted children, but it was impossible now. At least it was impossible to carry a baby. Not after her womb was destroyed by treatments and ripped from her body.

She heard what the doctor said.

She stood there for what seemed like forever, staring at the bright blue-eyed baby cooing in her arms. He was so beautiful it overwhelmed her to look at him. He was content in her arms, and she knew when Michelle got a feeling for it, she would love it.

Her eyes landed on a timid frame, tentative footsteps entering the room. Michelle looking pained and anxious, hunched over as if afraid to be seen.

"Hey, darling." Lucas stood to greet her.

"Hi," she breathed as she kissed him softly.

"You ready to go?" Jessica asked. "You go and get the stroller ready. I will wait here with Ryan."

Michelle looked relieved she didn't have to hold him just yet.

One step at a time, Jessica thought.

And that one step was all it took. Minutes into the walk and Michelle asked if she could take over and push the stroller.

She asked.

Like she needed permission to step into motherhood.

Jessica doubted just one walk would make everything perfect, but she hoped it was a start.

"He really is beautiful, isn't he?" Michelle whispered as she peered in on him, lying fast asleep.

"He's yours. Of course, he's beautiful."

"I don't think I have the confidence to do anymore but take him on walks right now, but I'm hoping it will come to me soon. Thank you."

"What are you thanking me for? This was all you."

"You've listened to me complain for over an hour. If it wasn't for you, I'd still be in bed. After Rob, it wouldn't have surprised me if you never wanted to see any of us again."

"I enjoyed listening to you complaining. I missed it," she teased, giggling as Michelle childishly stuck out her tongue. "But what Rob did to me has nothing to do with you or your family. I've always loved you all. I just couldn't face him for a while. Now, I'm stronger."

"I'm glad you came. Will you come in? I missed you so much. I'll make you a coffee and you can tell me everything. A proper catch-up."

Hardly, she thought.

It would drive the poor girl to her grave if Jessica started with her problems, too.

She halted at the door as Lucas came to open it.

"I really should get off, M. I'll call again next week. I promise."

Truthfully, she wanted to go home, go to bed, and allow herself to drown in her sorrows.

"Please do."

"I will."

"Thank you," Lucas whispered in her ear as she hugged him goodbye. She winked and nodded before saying her final farewells.

After almost an hour and a quick stop for coffee later, she arrived inside her apartment building; tired, hurt, and emotionally drained. Her legs ached as she climbed the stairs, cursing herself for not being patient enough to wait for the elevator. As she got to her floor, she searched through her bag for keys.

"Damn bag, why do I buy them so big?" she complained to herself. Half her day was always spent searching around in handbags.

"I always wondered that, too."

She shuddered, startled by the familiar tone. She looked up to see Jake's pained expression stare down at her from his powerful frame.

"Jake," she said casually, but inside her heart had stopped. "How was Katie?" she finally asked bitterly, tightening her hold around her keys.

"Jess," he breathed, and he was in front of her in one long stride, cradling her face in his hands.

For a fleeting moment, she almost succumbed to him. Then everything he said to her earlier came flashing back, washing over her in waves. Firmly, she placed her hand on his chest, stopping him from doing what he had in mind. Feeling his breath sweep across her face, she almost reached up to kiss him.

"Go home. Please," she pleaded, as the tears drained from her eyes. "I'm hurt, and right now, I can't forgive you. Give me time," she sighed before she backed away from his touch, walked inside to the warmth of her apartment, and turned to look back at him. "I'll see you at work, Jake."

It was for the best. At least now she didn't have to tell him she was sick.

Telling herself as much was the only way she knew how to comfort herself when she woke that night in a cold sweat. She reached over to the other side of the bed, forgetting he wasn't there. She gasped helplessly, searching over the empty ice-cold bed sheets. He wasn't there to hold her, or to make her feel safe.

He wasn't there.

Her breathing became hysterical as she clung to the sheets.

"Jake," she whispered, repeating his name until her tears soaked the satin pillow slip and her sobs became screams in her attempts to call out for him.

But, of course, he couldn't hear her.

EIGHTEEN

Jessica felt agitated Monday morning lying on her sofa. Her eyes were heavy, swollen, and brimmed red. When she looked at herself in the full-length mirror, she sighed inwardly at the state of her appearance. Sleep only came to her in waves, washing over her tired body in outbursts.

She dreamed about Jake for the time she slept. It was so real she could feel his touch along her skin and his breath against her cheeks. The reality of the dream didn't help though, because when she woke, only a cold, empty spot occupied her thoughts until she finally cried herself back to sleep somewhat two hours later.

Deep inside, she wanted to tell him she was sick. She wanted him with her today, going for the scan, but he went through it all with his mother. He saw her get sicker and sicker every day until she finally gave in.

She couldn't allow him to go through it again. She couldn't hurt him.

She called Sophie at the office and told her she wouldn't be in today. Acting out the fake sneezes and the odd, painful sniffle, she said, "Sorry Sophie, but would you be able to tell Mr. Johnson, or…" she swallowed and bit down on her dry, chapped lip, "Mr. Williams, I can't make it in today. I'm not feeling the best."

"No problem. I hope you're feeling better soon," Sophie said sympathetically.

Yeah, I hope I am too, she thought to herself before she ended the call.

She swallowed the tough lump forming in the back of her throat and focused her eyes on the talk show lively playing on the television screen. She didn't want to think of the way her stomach was churning and decorating itself with massive knots.

It was Monday.

Great, she thought to herself.

Another doctor's appointment, another smelly hospital, and yet another day in the life of Jessica Connors. Lord, she hoped things wouldn't get worse because her coping skills were faltering. She wanted to climb under a massive rock and not coming out until everything was exactly the way it was three months ago.

Her life was fine then. She wasn't sick. She didn't have a love life.

It didn't bother her until Jake came marching into her life with all guns blazing, showing her exactly what it was like to have a man touch her again. And how she loved it. At least she was honest enough to admit it to herself. She wasn't ashamed that Jake made her body do unpredictable things when he was around her.

She glanced at the clock again, throwing her head back and groaning.

She never knew time could go so slow. She tried to doze on the sofa for an hour to pass the time, but she didn't sleep. Instead, the ticking of the clock began sounding as if tiny explosions were erupting through her living room. She carried herself lazily to the bathroom, removed her old sweatpants and baggy jumper she wore going around the apartment, and turned on the shower. Thankfully, the balmy water relaxed her aching muscles.

Pity it couldn't do the same for her heart.

As she massaged the cherry shampoo into her scalp in slow and soothing motions, she let the aroma burst through her senses in a soft pour. Allowing her eyes to close for a moment, she removed her face from the heavy sprinkles of water and let them caress over her shoulders and down her back in silky movements. As she did, she felt her eyes fill with tears, heavy tears of loneliness. Helplessly, she leaned her back against the cold tiles of the shower, shivering as the icy drops left from the steam cradled her spine. She tried to wipe them away from her already wet cheeks, but fresh ones fell in their place.

How did she get here? How did she let herself get so involved?

Jessica closed her eyes for another long moment and let her sobs control her body as she slid down the shower wall and onto the floor, letting the water from overhead drown out her tears in complete defeat.

She thought of his eyes moving up and down her body. They were like dark chocolate; they were so brown. But they had a hint of gold in them when he looked down at her from his strong, tall frame. His muscular body made her feel like she was on fire with just a single glance, and his smile made her feel like there was nobody else in the world he cared about. Remembering his touch made her gasp there and then.

"Stop doing this to yourself."

Her eyes shot open.

Jessica dried her hair and, about satisfied with her appearance, she slipped her feet into her shoes, shuffled her arms into her black jacket, and wrapped her purple woolly scarf around her neck. It was 1.15 p.m., and it was a twenty-minute drive to the hospital, and considering the lunchtime traffic, she needed to get a move on.

Half an hour later, with the sound of honkers buzzing in her ears, she pulled up outside the hospital. Nervous and anxious, she strolled into the large building through the automatic glass doors. She took the elevator to the third floor, where her doctor's office was located.

Running her fingers through her loose curls, she massaged the bridge of her nose. A headache was forming behind her eyes. She couldn't blame this one on this medication. Nope. This was a Jake headache. A love headache. An *I-think-I'm-going-to-crack* headache.

Had she not learned from before that in her life, when it rained, it poured, and then a whole thunderstorm followed, maybe even a hurricane?

In the past, she always held on and fought through everything thrown at her. But right now, she wasn't so sure she could get through it.

That's because you need to tell somebody, a small voice rang in the back of her mind.

She huffed loudly, turning towards the large oak desk where an elderly nurse stood patiently behind it.

Yes, that voice was quite right. She needed to tell somebody. Jessica didn't have to go through this alone, and she had plenty of loving people around her who would be more than willing to help. She sighed inwardly, making the conscious decision to tell someone. Anybody but Jake, of course.

"Hello love, what can I do for you today?" The grinning, small, grey-haired receptionist beamed from across the desk.

"Hi." Jessica smiled back at her kindly. "I have an appointment with Doctor Harris."

The elderly lady smiled and gave a brief nod before she went to go through a pile of brown folders.

"Oh dear," she laughed, turning back to look at Jessica. "I forgot to ask your name." She blushed.

"Jessica Connors."

"Here we go," she said, pulling out Jessica's folder. "Take a seat, and Doctor Harris will be with you in a moment."

She smiled gratefully before taking a seat on the blue cushioned sofa opposite the desk. She was the only patient there in the spacious and intimidating waiting room. She flicked through several fashion magazines and read one or two articles, but none of them sunk in. Her mind was elsewhere, feeding her with even more nerve-wracking tingles.

"Jessica."

Her head popped up to see Doctor Harris' small frame standing over her. She hadn't even heard him coming.

"Would you like to come with me?" he asked, smiling so that his wobbly jaws turned upwards, making his eyes squint into what looked like tiny jewels.

"Of course."

"Ultrasound is this way. I'm sure you want to get this over and done with, so we can discuss your decision there."

He opened the door to a small room with a white leather bed and computer screen standing in the middle. There was no window, just a dim light shining from the ceiling.

"Pop up here." He patted the bed as he skimmed through her file. She removed her coat and scarf and placed them on a chair in the corner before pulling her body onto the cold bed. Sucking in a steadying breath, she inhaled the fresh smell of the room as he placed the folder on the table. "You look tired." He searched her face. "How have you been feeling?"

"I didn't get much sleep last night. It must have been nerves," she explained, leaving out the real reason she hadn't slept. "And apart from the headaches and nausea, things have been good. Nothing too serious."

"I sense you're not one to complain, Jessica." He eyed her. "This scan is so we can compare to previous ultrasounds. You will still need your MRI before we can proceed with any treatment. Though it's only precautionary. Your biopsy showed no positive margins. But don't worry. We'll take good care of you here at the hospital."

"I know," she murmured, fearful her voice would break. She watched as he switched on the machine, and it hummed to life. He fiddled with buttons before he turned to look at her.

"I know this is hard for you." He locked his fingers together. "But have you decided about treatment? I can only advise. The decision is yours."

Jessica swallowed away the fear and tears travelling to her eyes. She needed to be brave. Weakness was not an option.

"Yes," she answered firmly, her voice sounding more confident than she felt. "I still think a hysterectomy is the best option." She nodded her head, confirming her choice not only to the doctor but to herself.

"Well, I know it will stop you from ever giving birth, but it will be the most accurate, and hopefully we will remove all the cancer. And there are so many other ways of becoming a parent," he told her before giving her a gentle, supportive smile. "You're a very strong young woman," he complimented.

She didn't feel strong. It was all a front with her. Inside, she was emotionally dying. Jessica bit down on her lip and nodded her head.

"I can only do my best," she answered.

"Very true," he agreed, picking up a plastic bottle full of blue gel. After unbuttoning her jeans and lowering them in just the slightest, she lifted her shirt so he could do the scan.

She winced as the cold blue gel met her bare skin. Then he lifted what Jessica remembered from biology class as being a transducer probe and pressed it against the lower part of her stomach.

This was the part in the movies when they tell you how bad it is. Well, this didn't feel like a movie to her. Nope, this was as real as she was going to get it.

He pressed it harder for a long moment, moving it around until satisfied.

"Here we go," he trailed off, his small eyes narrowing on the screen.

He took a swift, deep breath and pressed harder against her stomach. She flinched as the pressure made her want to burst. Did he forget she had to have a full bladder for this ultrasound? If he didn't ease off on the pressure, he was going to be cleaning up after a very unpleasant accident.

"Oh my," he breathed, pressing even harder, and the entire colour drained from her cheeks.

"What is it?" she asked, swallowing away the knot of complete terror. "Is it worse than what you thought?"

He sat still for what seemed like forever, staring at the image on the monitor. He averted his gaze from the screen to look down at her, releasing the pressure from her stomach and wiping away the gel. His entire face looked like it cemented into a shocked expression.

"Doctor Harris?" she begged before he looked back at the screenshot he had taken.

"I think you should sit up," he advised. "I need to talk to you."

With shaking hands, she buttoned her jeans and pulled her top back over her bare skin, sitting up to look at his worried eyes.

"I'm guessing you don't know about this," he spoke mainly to himself. "Jessica, have you experienced anything odd going on with your body lately? Sickness, maybe?" he questioned. "Not being able to keep down anything you ate?" He listed the options.

"A little," she spoke reluctantly. "Once or twice, but nothing that stands out. I get nausea quite a lot, but you explained it's natural," she answered anxiously.

What the hell was going on?

"Of course," he said under his breath.

"Doctor Harris?"

"Jessica, just now, during the scan, I noticed," he stuttered, taking a deep breath to gather his thoughts. "I'm going to have to say this straight out."

"Then do it."

"Jessica, you're pregnant."

The world stopped moving.

Her vision blurred and the humming from the machine silenced.

Motionless for a moment, she stared at him, confused.

So terribly confused.

A tiny gasp of air escaped through her lips.

"I'm sorry, I'm what?" she blurted, feeling her stomach boil.

"You're pregnant," he repeated cautiously, staring at her as if she had just turned into another species. Or was that fear in his eyes?

"But… But… I didn't even think it was possible."

She bit down on her lip as her eyes widened. She didn't know what she was asking or thinking. He was wrong. He had to be. He *needed* to be wrong. There was no way she was pregnant. She couldn't be.

"Jessica, I said you couldn't get pregnant after the treatment, not before. The cancer is there, but you can still get pregnant. Nothing is preventing a pregnancy. Have you any idea of when your last period was?"

"I don't know. It's the reason I went to get my smear test. My periods were so irregular."

And she sat there feeling emotionless for a few moments. What was she supposed to say? How was she supposed to feel?

"Oh, my God." She finally found words in Christ. A single tear trailing down her cheek as her hand shot over her mouth, muffling her sounds. She wasn't even religious, but she felt the need to mutter a silent prayer. Someone had to help her.

"You need to calm down, because this is crucial. I don't mean to be rude, but do you know the father?" Doctor Harris questioned, concerned.

Of course, she knew the father. There was no one else it could be. She hadn't been with anyone else but Jake.

Oh God, here came the hurricane.

All she could do was nod her head robotically in response to his question.

"How do you think the father would react to this?"

She stared up at him, feeling numb.

"I don't know," she answered honestly. "He loves children."

He admitted he wanted children someday, but all he had to do was find the one worth fighting for. And if she were to trust what he said in the hotel two nights ago, then she was the one worth fighting for. He wanted *her* children.

"According to the scan, you're about 7 weeks pregnant. You understand that to go ahead with a hysterectomy or any kind of treatment, you will have to have a termination," he explained, taking her hand in his gentle touch.

"No," she said, exasperated, her eyes wide and furious. "I can't," she cried.

She couldn't terminate her this pregnancy. She received the chance to do something she thought was impossible, and he wanted her to get rid of her baby.

"Can't you do the operation after I give birth?" She heard something like that happening before.

"I don't know how fast this is going to spread. If it travels too far during the pregnancy, there is nothing I can do for you when the baby is born," he told her.

"But will the baby survive through it?"

"Your cancer, for now, is contained in the cervix. So yes, it's possible to give birth, but please Jessica, you must think seriously about this. The cancer is small enough for me to remove now. I can't promise that in seven months." His face seemed permanently stuck in worry mode. "This might be the only chance you have of life."

"It might be the only chance I have to give life," she corrected him.

"But what if something were to happen to you after the birth? Where will the baby go?"

She wiped away the endless tears streaming down her face, sniffing as the sobs shook through her body.

"I think I need to talk to Jake. He's the father. I need to speak to him before I decide."

Rubbing her flat stomach, Jessica didn't think she would have the strength to get rid of the life of her child in trade for her own, but if Jake wasn't willing to be a part of the baby's life if something were to happen to her, then there was no point leaving her child an orphan. And for all she knew, Jake could've wanted absolutely nothing to do with her.

She wanted him there with her, to hold her and to tell her everything was going to work out fine.

"With all due respect, Jessica, I don't think he will let you risk your own life for that of an unborn child."

She took a deep breath before speaking. "He doesn't know I'm sick," she told him, watching as his small eyes grew bigger. "And he won't. All I want to know is if he wants a baby with me or not."

"You can't possibly…"

"Yes, I can," she cut through.

He shook his head, his eyes still wide, his throat bobbing as he swallowed.

"I guess there's no point in me trying to talk more sense into you. You seem like a woman who will do what she believes is best. With or without medical advice," he pressed.

She wasn't listening to him anymore. He wasn't making sense to her. All she wanted to do was get out of the hospital and go straight to see Jake. This hurricane hitting her was a number nine on the Richter scale and looking to hit a number ten when she went to visit Jake.

"Jessica, you can't waste time with this. I need you to talk to the father tonight because you have to tell me your decision tomorrow and no later," he demanded before she left.

Her hands trembled as she opened the door of her car.

She pulled out her phone and tried calling Jake's. She wanted to meet him somewhere, but there was no answer.

"Why do you even have a phone?" she groaned.

Instead, she called his office and his new assistant answered, informing her that he, too, had taken the day off.

She drove as fast as she could to his house, praying to whoever was out there that he was home. Jake had given her the chance to be a mother, and he controlled whether to take it away from her. She wanted a baby so badly, even more so since she found out she would no longer be capable of conceiving, but she wanted Jake's baby. She wanted him to be the father of her child.

As she pulled up outside his large house, she forgot about everything he said to her the day before. It didn't matter anymore. There were far more important things to worry about.

Taking a deep breath to calm her failing nerves, she got out and carried her weak, heavy legs up the steps towards his front door.

His garden was beautiful, but only thanks to a gardener, and not his handy work. Two perfectly cut green areas decorated with brilliant, coloured flowers surrounded the steps leading to his red brick home. The leaves and petals swayed under the light mist and cool breeze.

Hesitantly, she lifted her hand and knocked on the wooden door.

Would he want the baby? Would he want her? How would he react?

"Come on, Jake," she muttered to herself as her leg started jolting again at an unnatural speed.

The door flew open to uncover his shocked face, staring at her. His wild eyes scanned her body, making the familiar heat radiate.

He was gorgeous, and it didn't help that he was standing there in just grey sweats, leaving his tanned muscular chest exposed.

"Fuck. Jess," he stuttered.

"Do you always answer the door like that?" She forced a smile, avoiding his reaction to her, while the tears floated in her raw eyes. She loved this man so much, and he didn't even know it.

"Sweetheart, come in," he trailed off as his eyes searched hers.

As her body trembled, he was in front of her in less than a second. He wiped away her heavy tears with his thumb, cradling her face in his hands.

"Hey, beautiful." He smiled, placing his fingers under her chin to tilt her face up to look at him. "What's wrong, Jess?" he asked softly.

"You're going to hate me."

"Hey, hey," he said frantically, trying to soothe her. "Don't you dare ever think that. Do you understand? That will never happen. You have no idea," he whispered as she stared up at him through bewildered eyes. "I'm insanely in love with every inch of you. I could never possibly hate you. I've been away from you less than twenty-four hours and I haven't slept thinking of what I said to you." He looked like he was in agony as he closed his eyes. "The mention of Rob's name sent me over the edge. Baby, I swear," he said, placing her hand in his and pressing it to his chest, "I will never hurt you again because if I ever see the same look in your eyes as I did yesterday, I don't think I could live with myself."

Her body shook as more sobs exploded through her shoulders in violent waves.

"Oh God, Jake," was all she could say when she thought of everything that was happening. And more tears fell. But before she could say anything else, he pulled her close, crushing her with the warmth of his body.

"It's okay, sweetheart. I'm here. I'll always be here. I won't let anything happen to you. You're safe. I've got you." He promised with whispered words as he kissed the top of her head.

She was where she wanted to be. This was her life.

He was her life.

She just hoped he was willing to accept something more.

NINETEEN

"Jake," Jessica finally managed to let his name escape her sobs.

Reluctantly, she pulled away from the heat of his bare flesh to wipe the tears from her sore eyes. He hadn't asked what was wrong yet, or why she was sobbing uncontrollably for the last five minutes. Instead, he stood there under the shelter of the porch and let her cry out whatever pain and fear she was feeling. She was shaking. She could feel it. She could feel her shoulders trembling against his firm grip as he placed his hands on her arms.

"Come on." Jake slipped his fingers down to her palms. "Let's get you inside." He wrapped his arm securely around her waist and guided her into the comfort and warmth of his home.

She'd been there before, many times, but never under the same circumstances.

Jake bought the then old and crumbling house two years ago, after his break-up from Katie. It would've been easier, and probably cheaper, for him to knock it down and rebuild it, but he didn't. He claimed he liked the character and feel too much.

The house felt different to her now as her shoes met the rich, dark wood floors in the hall. The long red and gold rug spread across the long hallway and matched the tall vase that stood, almost proudly, filled with gold branches in the corner beside the front door where they had entered.

Jessica smiled to herself then, because suddenly, the house

screamed '*home*.'

Nothing about the house ever seemed to be a bachelor pad, even with only Jake living there. Anybody that walked through his house for the first time would have thought he was a settled man with a wife and children to go home to.

It was thanks to April, who decorated the house, as she had done with Jessica's apartment. But this house was more like a palace compared to Jessica's small, shabby apartment in the city. Still, she couldn't help but feel proud of her younger sister. She was amazing at what she did, even if she was a complete and utter nutcase.

"Someday, it might be a long time down the road, but someday he is going to stop messing around and he is going to meet someone he wants to spend the rest of his life with, and she won't want to walk into a house that looks like a man's world. I'm only thinking ahead, for his sake," April had said.

How ironic, Jessica thought to herself.

Gently, he removed the strands of her dark auburn hair from her face and soothed her pale cheeks with his knuckles.

"I'm going to put a sweater on," he told her before planting a quick kiss on her lips and disappearing upstairs. She wanted to scream after him and demand he remain exactly where and how he was.

The brown carpet felt soft under her feet as she made her way into the living room. The dull light from outside was the only light filtering through the room and the drops of rain splattered on the window reflected on the cream walls. It seemed depressing and doing little to lift her dampened spirits. Too fitting. She shuddered before switching on the lamp and letting the light illuminate the room, giving it the warm and cosy feeling she always remembered it to have.

April had given him some freedom to embrace his manhood in this room. A large, wide-screen television placed on the wall overhead the set fireplace, topped off with a full surround sound system.

What always stood out, Jessica noticed, were the photos he had of his mother around the house. He did that all by himself. Very few photos littered the house, but the ones that did were the ones he held remarkably close to his heart. He was close to his mother, and it was a death Jessica doubted he ever got over. Probably never would.

Having been best friends with Jessica's mother since they were teenagers, her death was a major blow to both families. As an only child, his mother's death continued to haunt him.

"Are you okay?"

She jumped as Jake wrapped his muscular arms around her waist and pulled her closer to him. She shivered, as she always did when his body pressed against hers.

She was staring at his mother's picture when he pressed his chin against her shoulder. Secretly, she was wondering if their child would look like Catherine. She hoped so. Jake had gotten his attractive features from both sides, but he had his mother's eyes.

"You must miss her?" Jessica finally asked after a long moment's silence.

"Every day," he simply answered before trailing light kisses down her neck.

She turned to face him so his mouth covered hers, but before the moment could get too heated, she dragged her lips away from his, and with an apologetic smile she took a deep breath, noticing how he was wearing a navy sweatshirt now.

"Jake," she said, filling her lungs with air, her courage faltering with each passing second. "I think you should sit down. I need to tell you something." She swallowed hard.

What was she supposed to say to him? How was she going to tell him this without breaking down completely? And what if he told her he wanted nothing to do with the child?

His eyes narrowed and searched her face intensely, but she looked away from the complete fear and worry that had taken over his expression.

"Jess," he almost begged in a bare whisper.

"Please sit down," she told him, unable to meet his gaze. She wasn't so sure the knot in her stomach would hold on and let her survive.

Ugh, her mouth was beginning to water.

Thankfully, he obeyed and went to sit on the sofa. He didn't sit into it, though. He sat on the edge. Exactly how she felt.

She let her eyes glance at him a few times before she sat in the chair on the opposite side. Only the large coffee table separated them. But she wished it didn't because she felt like he was miles away. Looking down at her lap, her hands were trembling uncontrollably, and no number of deep breaths were going to stop it.

"I went to the doctor's today," she finally said, looking up at him, sensing he was going to say something if she didn't. Heavy tears glossed over her eyes, but she lowered her head to hide it. "Jake, I don't want to pressure you into anything, and I'll understand if you want nothing to do with it."

But he cut her off then, getting up from his chair to touch her face.

"Jess, you're killing me. Please tell me what is wrong?"

She closed her eyes for a brief second and took a long, deep breath.

Just tell him.

"Jake. I'm… I'm pregnant," she finally said, staring straight at him and letting the tears leak.

Lord, he was going to hate her.

He didn't do anything. He didn't move. He didn't flinch. And she swore for a long moment, he didn't breathe. But all too quickly, his hands slipped from her face, falling to his sides.

Defeat clawed its way inside, her shoulders rounding forward on a long exhale, and her heart shattered. Every second he remained silent, he stole another piece of her fractured spirit, and kept them for himself.

Miles. It's how far he was staring. Straight through her like a knife.

"Jake, please say something," she begged, her voice breaking, and every breath was painful to take. She knew deep inside that the words that would eventually flow from his mouth could continue to break her or take all those pieces and put them back together.

But to her amazement, he simply smiled. The corner of his mouth edged, and his eyes welled.

"I'm going to be a father," he stated slowly, like he needed time for the words to sink in, and his voice was thick with emotion.

"Yes," she choked.

"You're going to be a mother?"

"Yes," she repeated.

"You're having my baby? We're having a baby?"

Jesus.

"Yes," she laughed through tears, not sure what else to say.

He blinked hard. And again.

His chin quivered.

Oh, Jake.

"Baby, you're going to be the most perfect mother." His smile widened and her heart swelled in her chest.

"And you…" She leaned forward, resting her palm on his cheek. "You are going to be a perfect father."

Gasping loudly, she looked down to see he had lightly pressed his palms against her stomach.

"You're carrying my baby in there. Our baby."

She didn't want to wake up because she was sure this was a dream. He leaned in and kissed her. He kissed her like the first time, like the last time, like the world would end and it wouldn't matter.

"I was so scared you would walk away from me." He rubbed his fingers over her lips. "But now, you've no other choice but to stay and I don't care if I'm being selfish, because goddamn it, I love you."

Her heart was going to explode now, she was sure of it.

"Jake, even if I had a choice, I would never walk away. I don't think I ever could. This..." She placed his hand on her chest, right over her heart, and she knew he could feel it beat frantically. She didn't care. "This is yours. You can have it all because I have already given it to you. I was so scared that you were going to be angry..."

"Angry?" he blurted in disbelief. "This baby, if it is at all possible, only makes me love you more." He laughed gently as he wiped the endless falling tears from her vulnerable face. In one swift movement, he tossed her arm around his neck and leaned in.

"What the hell are you doing?" she screeched through her laughter as he swept her up into his arms and headed towards the stairs.

"I'm going to remind you exactly how we made this kid."

Then, ever so carefully, as if scared he might break her, he placed her in the center of the large bed and his sturdy frame hovered above her.

She wanted nothing more, so it felt like forever before he slowly leaned down and kissed her.

TWENTY

Jessica's muscles ached as she tried to push open her eyelids and move her stiff limbs. The room was dark when she finally managed to open her eyes and, looking at the clock on the bedside locker, she sighed. It was 6:30 a.m. She would have to get up soon and go about life as normal. She never wanted to leave the warmth of Jake's arms. It felt like home to her. She smiled in a relaxing breath and hugged Jake closer. Butterflies swarmed around as she remembered what happened yesterday. It felt like she was in a dream, and someone was going to come along and wake her.

Was it even possible to be this happy? A short few months ago, she never would've thought of her and Jake together in a romantic relationship. Having a civil conversation with him then was torture. Now, she was carrying his child and so madly in love with him.

She tilted her head up to look at him sleeping for a moment, before kissing him gently on the lips and quietly getting out of bed, careful not to wake him. She grabbed one of his large t-shirts from his wardrobe and pulled it over her head, so it feathered the bare flesh of her thighs. Creeping to the bathroom, she splashed some cold water on her face and brushed her teeth.

When she returned, she was greeted by the bewildered and tired eyes of Jake as he sat up and leaned against the pillows.

"You're awake?" she stated, smiling gently as she tilted her body against the door frame and crossed her arms under her chest.

"I thought you'd left." He yawned, rubbing his hands over his face. *He looked cute when he was tired*, she thought.

"No, I'm right here," she assured him, making her way towards the bed and crawling beside him so she was lying on her stomach and waving her legs in the air behind her.

"My sweater suits you." He eyed her body with mischievous eyes. Her cheeks flushed a soft pink.

"Yeah, I'm sorry. It gets worse." She flinched. "I used your toothbrush."

He kissed her softly. "My toothpaste tastes nice," he commented, leaning back with a satisfied grin on his face. "Me and you." He waved his finger between them both. "We are taking the day off today. I called your boss. He said to take as long as you need."

"I should thank my boss. I wonder how I could do that."

"I may have a few ideas."

"Hmm, I'm sure you do, but don't you have a big meeting this morning?"

"I can cancel the meeting. You're more important."

"As much as that touches my heart." She climbed up on the bed to sit beside him, letting her folded legs fall onto his stomach. "You can't cancel that meeting. You know this is for you, and besides, I have things to do today. Not that you're not important, but I promised Michelle I would visit and see how she is doing."

Truthfully, she needed to take a trip to her doctor and let him know about her decision to keep the baby.

"I'll call by later," she promised.

"You shouldn't have to just call by," he said, sounding serious now, his gaze focused straight ahead. She followed his eyes to the wall.

"You okay in there?"

He seemed deep in concentration, and as if he had suddenly made a revelation, his eyes widened.

"Jake?" she whispered, totally baffled.

He didn't reply.

"Jake?"

"Move in with me," he blurted, looking at her now.

"What?"

"Move in with me," he repeated. "If we're going to make a go of this, we should do it right."

"Is it not too soon?"

"Baby, I have known you all your life."

"Jake, I don't—"

"What are you scared of?"

She thought for a moment and lowered her eyes.

"Nothing," she finally answered, feeling the tears soak her lashes.

"I want you to be here. I want to look at you when I choose and say I love you when I choose. I don't want to go through the torture of yearning after you. I want to look after you, like I should be. And you shouldn't have to visit me. I want you to call this your home because I don't want to love you when you are halfway across town. I want to love you when you are here, next to me."

"I love you."

There it was. She said it and there was no going back. She was his for the taking. An intense and meaningful expression flickered through his dark chocolate eyes.

"You have no idea how much." He took her face in his hands and placed his lips over hers.

Coming up for some well-deserved air, she climbed in between his legs, waiting for her heartbeat to go back to normal. Somehow, she doubted it ever would. He enveloped his arms around her abdomen and tugged her closer to the warmth of his body while she let her head fall back onto his shoulder.

"I think it's going to be a boy." He kissed her cheek.

"Another you? The poor girls," she teased, giggling as he puckered his brow and glared at her.

"We're going to have to tell our families soon enough."

Jessica grunted. "That should be fun. My brother is going to love you after that."

"Please, Jess, don't remind me."

"I have to tell Sharon," she wailed.

"Good luck to you," he whispered frigidly.

"Hey, I didn't make this baby myself. It takes two to tango."

"And I am so grateful you tangoed with me." He smirked, kissing the bare skin of her neck. "But I'm leaving Sharon for you."

"Chicken shit," she mocked.

"And proud," he added. "So, when are you going to move in?"

"I think we should wait until we tell our families, at least."

"I suppose we should," he agreed, disappointment edging his features. "But from now to then, would you like to make your visits very long ones?"

"You sound desperate," she joked.

"This is what you do to me."

***

Four hours later, Jessica sat in her car on the way to see her doctor. She practically pushed Jake to work, and even then, he sulked.

She went home for a quick shower and called the hospital. Doctor Harris agreed to see her that morning. He wasn't going to be thrilled with her decision, but it was her life, and this was best for her. It was a bonus that she made Jake happy along the way.

She was going to tell him about the cancer and knew exactly when.

"Jessica." Doctor. Harris' small, rounded frame hovered over her. She hadn't even noticed him standing there. "Would you like to step into the office?"

"Of course." She nodded, embarrassed by her dazed state.

Yesterday, when she walked into a room similar to this, she was so nervous about finding out how bad her situation was. Now, she was excited to tell him that, even though she may lose her own life, she could give somebody else theirs.

"Jessica." He intertwined his fingers on the desk after a moment. "I know what happened yesterday must have been difficult for you, and I'm sorry you couldn't have more time to think about it."

"That's okay," she assured him. "I had my mind made up before I even left the hospital, so it took little convincing on my part."

"You've made your decision." He shifted uneasily in his chair. "And you've spoken to the father about the situation?"

"Yes. He wants this baby as much as I do." She beamed, still not believing Jake was so excited about the pregnancy. She was still waiting for someone to shake her and tell her it wasn't real.

"Oh." Doctor Harris looked away from her. "And of course, you told him about the cancer, right?"

Was she that obvious? She lowered her head to fight meeting his dubious gaze. In response, she merely shook her head.

"Jessica, you must tell him. He has to realize the consequences of you having this child."

"But you don't even know what the consequences are yet," she corrected him.

"Yes, you're right, but something tells me he wouldn't want to wait that long to find out. He has to know that in exchange for this baby's life, you could give your own."

"I'm not killing my child," she insisted. The notion of it sent chills through her body.

"But you're killing yourself instead." Composing himself then, he said, "Jessica, you need to tell him."

"I will."

He relaxed then. "When?"

She exhaled loudly. "When I'm five months pregnant," she answered him confidently. This was her plan, and nobody was going to get in the way.

His brows furrowed, bemused by her answer. "When you're five months," he trailed off and his eyes widened. "You want to wait until it's too late to end the pregnancy?" He finally realized. "Jessica, you could be making the biggest mistake of your life here."

"Could be, but I'm willing to take the risk, and nothing is going to change my mind."

"I can see that."

"I know you think I'm completely insane, but being a mother is what I want. I want to give birth to my baby, and now I know if anything happens to me, I'm leaving my child with the best possible person—its father."

"Well, as you said, this is your life, and I'm only your doctor. I'm only supposed to support and help you through whatever decisions you make. I just find it hard to understand, because I have three daughters of my own and the thought of losing them isn't even worth thinking about. The same goes for my wife. But if you are sure, I will have nothing more to say but words of encouragement."

She smiled gratefully. "Thank you."

"You know, strangely, I respect you. You're doing all of this on your own, and that takes a very brave person. And you're risking your life for the person you love most so that they can be happy. I may not understand it completely, but it doesn't mean I can't see your courage." He nodded towards her respectfully.

She didn't know how to respond. She didn't feel courageous or brave. She felt weak and feeble, but the hope for her unborn child kept her going. And she was going to make the most of her time with Jake and show him exactly how much she loved him. For all she knew, she might not have long left with him.

With another few minutes of small talk, Jessica stood and made her way towards the door.

"Take care of yourself." Doctor Harris patted her back as he opened the door. "And I'll have someone call you sometime this week to give you a follow-up appointment. If you have any problems, just call. You have my number, so don't hesitate."

"Thank you."

She was about to continue, but a soft voice interrupted.

"Doctor Harris."

Jessica turned to see a tall woman with prominent cheekbones and piercing olive-green eyes. She also noticed the sky-blue bandanna she wore around her head. She was beautiful, even without the long, flowing hair Jessica imagined she once had.

"Rachel," he exclaimed. "How lovely to see you again. You look like you're recovering well."

"I've never felt better." She smiled, exposing her perfect white teeth.

"There you are," a tall man raised his voice from further down the hall.

"It looks like your husband has been looking for you." Doctor Harris chortled, pointing in the man's direction.

Jessica turned her gaze to where the man was making his way towards them, and how she remained standing she would never know. Her mouth went dry, and her pulse shot through the roof.

She knew that face all too well. Standing next to his wife, he finally acknowledged her, and his reaction reflected hers.

"Jessica?" he breathed, shocked.

"Mark," she greeted him as the fear took hold of her limbs and made them feel like steel blocks.

The last thing she needed was to bump into the new guy from work. Even if she wanted to lie, she couldn't. Doctor Harris was the gynaecologic oncologist.

"Shit," she cursed, mentally handing herself a shovel to dig herself a bigger hole.

TWENTY-ONE

The next day, Jessica sat in her office, winding her hair around her fingers while tapping the other hand against her desk. She ran out of the hospital so fast yesterday she probably left skid marks across the white tiles. She hadn't planned on having anybody else know about her illness. It turned out that fate had a different plan.

"Take a deep breath," she told herself while filling her lungs with cramped office air. She needed to go outside and calm the erratic nervous system threatening to fail on her at any minute. Fresh air was exactly what she needed.

Bumping into Mark was not, but again, fate had a different plan.

"Jessica," he called.

Could she pretend she didn't hear him?

For the love of all that is holy, you work with the man. Telling herself otherwise and brainwashing herself would not work; no matter how hard she tried. If it didn't work with Jake, it wouldn't work this time.

"Hey, Mark." She turned on her heels.

"How are you feeling?"

There it was. The sympathy and puppy dog eyes. Everything she was trying her best to avoid.

"I'm great. Why wouldn't I be?" Jessica asked casually, letting his last remark shrug from her shoulders.

His eyebrows furrowed in confusion, and his long fingers automatically rose to run them through his black hair. She was making him feel like he was an idiot. She didn't want that. It was times like this she wished she had a stony heart.

"Look," she breathed, searching around to make sure nobody was there, "I'm all new to this, so I would appreciate it if you didn't breathe a word. I don't want people walking on eggshells because of the sick girl at work."

"I won't say anything. My wife was like you. She didn't want anybody to know, so I won't tell a soul. I promise you that."

"Thank you." She smiled gratefully.

"Jessica, if you need anybody to talk to, I'm here. My wife has been through this, and she knows what it's like. I'm sure she would be more than happy to talk to you."

"That is very kind of you, but I'm sure I'll be fine."

He searched her face for a moment. "Sometimes, it's good to talk to someone else other than your family. Families take it differently, and sometimes they're not always there when you need them. I can only imagine what your family must be going through. Even though my wife and I separated, she's a good friend, and she had me to support her the whole way through."

She watched him as he stood there in front of her and waited for her to answer. But what could she say? She just hoped the helplessness she felt wasn't written on her face.

"You told your family, right?"

Was she that easy to read?

She swallowed hard, feeling the lump in her throat grow bigger with each passing second. What was she supposed to tell him? Her answer was blank. She couldn't say anything.

"You haven't told them," he screeched.

"Be quiet!" She jumped, waving her hands in an attempt to shut him up. She didn't want the whole place knowing. "Right now…" She inhaled a deep breath. "You are the only person who knows. And I would like to keep it that way, if you don't mind."

"You mean you've told nobody? Jessica, you can't do this on your own."

"I beg to differ," she fought back, biting down on her glossy lip.

"Are you completely insane?"

"Probably," she answered, shrugging the shoulders that felt like they were carrying the weight of the world. "I have my reasons."

"What kind of reasons results in you battling cancer on your own?"

"Will you please keep your voice down?" she hissed through gritted teeth. He had no right to judge her. He had no idea what she was going through.

"I know this is probably none of my business, but it's obvious you and Jake are now together. Have you told him?"

Her eyes widened. "You're right. It's none of your business," she fumed before she turned and stormed off through the hallway towards the elevator.

But because of her lack of good luck, the elevator was already on the top floor, ten flights above her, and it was stopping on every single floor on the way down.

"Wait a minute."

Was her day going to get any worse?

"Please Mark, just drop it."

"No, I won't, because I have seen my wife go through this, and I almost lost her many times. I don't want to sit back and watch another man go through what I did when he doesn't even know what the hell is going on." His voice was getting louder with each syllable.

Now her head was spinning like crazy. She could feel the beads of perspiration crawl evilly down her back, making her shiver violently.

"Look, I'm going to tell him. Just not now," she breathed, her lungs searching for air. Her breathing escaped in loud gasps, her headache crippling.

"Jessica?" Mark's voice was distant and blurry. His warm grip around her upper arm steadied her somewhat until another familiar voice broke through.

"What's going on?"

Deep breaths, deep breaths, she reminded herself repeatedly.

"Jess?" It was from Jake. His panicked voice sent chills down her back. She needed to get a grip. "I've got you. Don't worry."

Her entire weight was leaning on him, relying on him for his support.

Opening her eyes, the hallway seemed to stand still, and her frantic heartbeat was regulating.

"I'm fine," she let out slowly, trying her best to stand up straight, but she failed and fell against Jake's body once again.

"I'm taking you to the doctor."

"No," she almost screamed. "I'm not going to the doctor."

"Jess, there could be something wrong with the…" He stopped

himself then and looked at Mark, remembering if he went any further, he would reveal the pregnancy.

She was standing there with two men, both knowing something about her the other didn't.

"There's nothing wrong, Jake," she pressed, relieving him of her weight as she pushed back on her heels.

"Do you need me to do anything?" Mark asked. Helplessness drenched his violet eyes.

"I don't need anybody to do anything. I am going to be fine." She darted a look at Jake, who still had his arm wrapped firmly around her waist. "Mark, you can get back to work."

"Okay. Go home and get some rest."

Jake turned to her when Mark left, and the look on his face made her eyes sting with heavy tears. He brushed her hair away from her face and feathered his fingers across her tender lips.

"Sweetheart, I really think you need to see a doctor."

"I don't need a doctor," she persisted. "It's morning sickness."

"You're so damn stubborn sometimes. Well, if you won't go to a doctor, I'm taking you home."

"I have work to do."

"You don't have a hope in hell. I'll carry you home if I have to. You know I will. And you can kick and scream all you like, but you need to take care of yourself."

He was right. It wasn't just about her anymore.

"Fine," she huffed. "Take me home."

Thirty minutes later, Jessica was wrapped up in Jake's bed.

"Since when does this become home?" she asked as he closed the curtains, blocking out the dull light from outside.

"Since I asked you to move in with me and you agreed," he affirmed casually, before strolling to her side and kissing her softly on the mouth. "I'm going to leave and let you get some rest."

"Oh, no you don't." She caught his arm before he had a chance to walk away. "If I have to be stuck in bed all day, then you have to be stuck here with me."

He chuckled loudly and then hesitated before rolling his heavenly eyes and removing his shoes to get in beside her. "You're taking the whole *we're* pregnant thing a little too far."

She snuggled into his warmth and embraced the feel of his body against hers.

"The things I do for you," he whispered close to her ear and kissed the top of her head. "You're lucky I love you."

"Yeah, I suppose I am," she breathed before she closed her eyes to sleep.

5 Weeks Later…

"Wake up!" Jessica shivered as he removed the blankets from her body, and cool air swept over her.

"Go away and leave me to sleep." She groaned, stretching her limbs.

"Stop stretching. It's not good for the baby."

"Shut up." She half-opened her eyes to see him fully dressed and brooding over her like she was some sort of unknown species.

"You have your scan today. Twelve weeks. We get to see that baby of ours, so get your ass out of bed and get dressed."

"Ugh," she groaned, throwing her legs over the side of the bed. "You know I hate you right now."

"Be careful using that word. It has a strong emotion attached to it. Have a shower and get dressed." He pushed her into the bathroom, slapping her ass as he closed the door.

"Prick," she hissed.

"I heard that," he shouted.

"I meant you to."

Jessica showered quickly, letting the almost scalding water and the smell of her cherry shampoo soothe her aching bones. Hopefully, the morning sickness would stay away.

And her positive thinking worked for once, considering they made it all the way to the hospital without once throwing up. That was a record. Usually, the baby didn't give her a break in the mornings.

Oh, and the smell of eggs. All she had to do was smell them, and her head was plunged into a toilet bowl for half the morning.

"What are you thinking about?" Jake quizzed as they pulled into an empty space outside the hospital.

She gagged. "Eggs," she answered, swallowing the bile rising in her throat.

"Why do you do this to yourself?"

She shrugged, asking herself the same question. She was putting herself through torture without even realizing it. But the poor little liquid chicks.

She gagged instantly.

"Jess, stop talking about the eggs, and don't puke in my car."

"Gee, thanks for the support."

"No problem." He flashed a wide smile at her before getting out to open her door.

"I can open my own car door. I'm only pregnant."

"I'm being supportive." He threw her words back at her and smiled smugly.

"Do me a favour. Be supportive and push this baby out for me when the times comes. If it has your head, it's only fair."

He rolled his eyes, ignoring her taunt. "Come on, beautiful. Get your sexy ass out of the car."

He took her hand as they strolled inside.

"You know, you won't be saying that in a couple of months, when my ass is the size of a small island."

"I don't care if your ass takes over the entire bed," he laughed, nudging her playfully.

She grimaced.

Once they got inside, Jessica gave her name to the receptionist and took her seat as she waited for the doctor to call her name. Doctor Harris was going to conduct the ultrasound, and she did everything in her power to make him promise not to say anything. He couldn't anyway because of confidentiality, but she still had to be sure.

"Jessica Connors," a familiar deep and jolly voice called. His small, smiling eyes awaited her as she approached him.

"Hey, Doc." She smiled gently.

"And you must be the father." He turned to Jake as they made their way into the ultrasound room.

"Jake Williams, nice to meet you." He gestured his hand and Doctor Harris shook it firmly, in the way only men could.

They seemed to eye each other sceptically for a moment. What was it with men and their constant ego battle? Jake was a God of a man, and Doctor Harris, although a nice man, was a blob. There was no competition there.

"You ready to see this baby?"

Jessica's stomach knotted with nerves and anxiety.

"Can't wait."

She pulled herself onto the leather bed and pulled her sweater up under her bra. She flinched as the gel squirted onto her bare flesh. He searched around for a long moment until a bright smile trapped his facial features.

"There it is." He pointed to a blurry area on the screen.

And then it came into focus.

Little hands and feet jerking around in sudden movements. And the most beautiful outline of a little face.

Jake's hand tightened around hers, and she felt his lips press softly to her forehead.

"We made that," he whispered.

"Yeah, we did," she agreed, letting the tears fall from her eyes as she turned to look at him.

"I love you," he mouthed silently.

She smiled then and let the joy take hold of her emotions. She didn't want to think about the bad things that lay ahead. This was their moment, and she was going to hold on to it for as long as she could.

"Always," she breathed, pulling him into her kiss. Breaking away, she glanced back at the screen and cringed.

"What is it?" Jake asked.

She cried. Not fake tears. Not happy tears. Real fat heavy ones.

"Jess, is this some sort of emotional pregnancy thing?"

"No," she choked, scrubbing her palms across her face. "It has your head."

TWENTY-TWO

"Are you nervous?" Jake's voice knocked her out of oblivion.

They were on their way to her parent's house and her stomach felt like it was twisting with a thousand knots as her leg bounced continuously up and down in the front seat.

"Yeah," she breathed, nodding her head without so much as glancing at him.

How were they going to react to this? Her parents meant so much to her. They didn't even know she and Jake were dating, let alone that she was pregnant with his baby.

"Calm down, Jess." He placed a firm hand on her knee to stop her leg from trembling. "Your brother took it well."

"Yes, after he called you every scumbag under the sun," she reminded him. "They don't even know we're going out, Jake, and now I have to jump right in there and tell them I'm pregnant."

It pained her to even say it. She didn't want to disappoint anyone; least of all her parents, but they needed to do it. She just wished someone else would do it for her.

"Sorry." She swallowed hard, turning to look at him now, regretting her outburst. It wasn't his fault. Well, maybe it was, but she didn't want to be angry with him.

She sat there and watched how his jaw flinched and his teeth gritted together as he saw the pain and worry in her eyes. It was something he had been trying to protect her from all her life. She just never knew it until recently. She smiled at him reassuringly, closing her eyes briefly before she whispered the words that flowed so freely from her mouth.

"I love you."

He smiled then and turned his head back towards the road.

"I love you, too."

Ten minutes later, they pulled into the driveway of her parent's house. She never knew the house she grew up in could look so daunting.

"Let's do it." Jessica was hoping her fearless body language would rub off on her erratic emotions.

"Sweetheart, what a lovely surprise." Her mother greeted her with a warm hug. Her eyes narrowed as she pulled away and set her confused gaze on Jake. "Did you two come over here together?"

Jessica swallowed hard and relaxed again as Jake soothed his hand over her back.

"We did," she answered, her voice reflecting the fear burning in her blue eyes.

"Well, come in. Don't just stand there."

"Is Dad here, Mom?"

"Yes sweetie, he's in the living room."

"Can I talk to you both?"

Jessica thought it best if she got straight to the point. There was no way she could survive through an entire conversation and the weekly gossip with her mother without her knowing there was something wrong. She was trembling with nerves, and Jake wasn't the only one who noticed.

"Of course," Rose responded quickly, her brows furrowing with more confusion.

As they made their way into the living room, Jessica greeted the smiling eyes of her father with a wide grin and a hug she never wanted to escape from. She wanted to stay there forever and be his little girl. It was exactly what she was dreading most about this conversation. Seeing her father's face was going to kill her or make her the proudest woman in the world.

She'd witnessed his unforgiving stare, and a whole month of the silent treatment when she was fourteen and had sneaked out of the house to be with a boy—not that they were doing any more than holding hands, but fathers' minds wander sometimes to a place where they can only see the danger.

She was caught, and she never heard from that boy again. Apart from the odd glance in history class, he never seemed to stare at her for more than five seconds because of the forever engraved visual of her father's rant that night.

"Are you all right, love? You're gone as pale as a ghost." Her father feathered his fingers along her ice-cold cheek.

Of course, she wasn't all right. She was about to tell her parents she was pregnant by a man they didn't even know she was dating.

"I'm fine," she assured him. Her lips were trembling as her best efforts failed to slide them into a soft smile.

"Will you both sit down, please?" She swallowed hard, taking a seat on the sofa opposite them.

She couldn't shake her mother's scrutinizing stares as she placed her body into the soft cushions of the sofa. Her mother's eyes could see right through her, and she knew something was up.

"Breathe," Jake whispered, quickly winking his eye.

She thought she was going to pass out as beads of sweat crept down her back, making her shiver violently.

"Mom. Dad." Jessica searched both of their faces and prayed the ground would just open up and swallow her.

"Are you two going out?" Rose blurted, straightening her back to sit up straight as she clasped her hands on her lap, tilting her head sideways as she waited for an answer.

Jessica didn't know what to say. It felt like her words had gotten stuck in her throat and she was unable to find them.

"I mean," her mother continued, her eyes shifting between them both repeatedly. "You arrived here together, which, not so long ago, would have been like drawing blood from a turnip. And you've been getting along better than you usually do. I noticed it the last time we all had dinner together."

Jessica turned to look at Jake, who seemed as helpless as she was.

"Is your mother correct?" her father interrupted.

"I'm right. Just look at them both."

Before Jessica could respond in any sort of way, Jake tore his eyes away from hers to her parents.

"Yes Rose, you're right."

She watched him smile proudly as he took her hand in his.

She felt numb. She hadn't even opened her mouth, and everything she feared was unfolding there in front of her. But there was no screaming and shouting, and people telling her how none of this was going to work. And before she had a chance to digest any of it, she became wrapped in her mother's arms, listening to her express her congratulations to them both.

"Your mother would be so proud of you, Jake." Rose hugged him tightly.

"Once you treat her well." Her father huffed. "I don't have a problem with it. Congratulations to you both."

"Thanks, Chris." Jake smiled; his voice full of relief.

And then she heard her mother go off again. She continued to rant and rant and rant about how lovely a couple they both make.

"And there I was thinking you were coming here to tell me something extreme. You looked like you had the weight of the world on your shoulders," Rose rambled on as Jessica sat there frozen in place, trying her hardest not to concentrate on her mother's lips move at the speed of light.

They still had to tell her parents the most important bit, but with her mother babbling on the way she was, they would never get the chance. She would have to deliver the baby in their living room.

"But our Jessica always was a worrier," she continued. "I'm so happy..."

"I'm pregnant," Jessica exclaimed, followed by a loud and painful gasp. It wasn't meant to come out that way, was it?

It shut her mother up if nothing else.

"Oh," was the only thing her mother could say.

"Yes, oh." Jessica nodded, feeling her cheeks burn.

She should have left her to her rant. And by the way Jake was darting looks at her, he thought the same thing.

"Now that nobody is saying anything, I'll tell you everything. I am three months pregnant with Jake's baby. And we're not just dating, we've been going out for months now, and we've moved in together."

"Holy mother of God." Her mother always went a little Catholic when shocked. "A little fast, don't you think?" Her mother's eyes narrowed into tiny lines.

"Probably, but we're doing this."

Her father spoke then, his lip twitching, "So, you got my daughter knocked up?"

"Dad!" Jessica warned, feeling the blood pound behind her ears.

She didn't dare look at Jake for fear she might pass out with just the look in his eyes.

Her mother didn't say anything. Maybe she was quietly hyperventilating. God knew Jessica was.

"You know," Chris began, a smile edging on his thin lips, "This would be a whole lot worse if you were a stranger, Jake. But it's not like you're going anywhere. You're already part of this family, so even if things don't work out between you and Jess, I know you'll still be there for this child."

Her eyes almost popped out of her head.

"I love your daughter, and no matter what, I will be there for my child. Things will work out for us. I know it."

Jessica looked towards her mother.

"Mom, are you okay?"

She was more than okay, and she proved it when she laughed herself into hysterics. Jessica hoped she was laughing because she was happy and not because she was about to choke her daughter.

"You sure know how to surprise your mother." Rose leaped up from the seat, and looking around, Jessica noticed the scared look in her father's eyes mirrored that of the terrified one in hers. "I'm proud of you, sweetie." Rose knelt beside Jessica and held her face in her hands.

"What? For getting myself knocked up?" Jessica teased, her nerves on the brink of giving up.

"Don't put it like that. You have a new life growing inside you and your father is right. It's not like Jake can go anywhere. And he wouldn't. I can see he loves you. He has loved you for an awfully long time." Rose smiled, staring at them both with so much adoration. "Congratulations to both of you. A baby is a blessing," Rose said before she kissed Jessica softly on the cheek.

***

The next morning, Jessica sat at her desk, sorting through a pile of books she had to get through by the end of the month.

"You're pregnant?"

Jessica jumped, her body shaking as her head shot up to the strong, tense figure of Mark standing at her doorway as his voice stormed through her room.

Her mouth suddenly became dry, and her hands cramped into fists.

"How the hell do you know that?" She stumbled over her words, trying to swallow away the terror in her voice.

"Your boyfriend is telling people," he said, stepping into her office, closing the door, and taking a seat in the chair opposite her.

"He's what?" Jessica bellowed, unable to find the strength in her legs to stand up. They hadn't discussed that part.

Mark rolled his irritated eyes and shook his head in disbelief.

"You're not getting my point here. You're pregnant," he repeated. "Jake is doing what every other proud father-to-be would do. Believe me, I know better than anyone how it feels. But I also have a good idea of what it feels like to know the person you love the most could be dying. But he doesn't know that part, does he?"

She took a deep breath, looking around the room, refusing to meet his steady gaze.

"You're scared in case he wants you to get rid of it, aren't you?"

"He wants this child more than anything else."

"In exchange for your life? I don't think so."

Jessica wiped away the moisture stinging her eyes.

"I know how this works, Jessica. My wife is in recovery, remember? Now that you're telling people, you must be around the three months stage."

She didn't answer. All she could do was stare at him and feel so helpless it felt like she was going to slide right off her chair to curl up into a ball on the floor.

"I get you want to see this child being born. But what if it's too late, and in exchange for your child's life, you give your own?"

"Exactly. It's *my* child. Mark, you have two kids, right? Don't tell me you wouldn't give your life for them in a split second."

She had him. She knew by the look in his eyes. She hit a soft spot.

"That doesn't excuse what you're doing to Jake. I can't sit back and watch a man go on about his life, not knowing that the woman he loves is going through the hardest time in hers, and he doesn't know about it. I can't imagine my wife going through what she went through without telling me."

Her breathing became suddenly frantic. What did he mean? He couldn't just sit back?

"What are you saying, Mark?"

"I'm saying that if you don't tell him, I will."

TWENTY-THREE

Jessica couldn't feel anything. She was waiting for someone to come along and tell her it was all a dream. Mark couldn't be serious, could he? He wouldn't tell Jake.

Who did he think he was? This was none of his business. Did he expect her to just crumble right there in front of him?

"You can't honestly tell me you are serious about this, can you?" She bit down on her already throbbing lip to stop herself from shouting the place down.

"And you can't honestly expect me to sit back and watch you go through this alone? The man you love is upstairs telling people you two are official, and he is about to be a father - an enormously proud one, may I add. Do you honestly think it's fair to him and expecting the mother of his child to be there through this?"

Mark closed his eyes briefly as he took a deep breath, sitting back in his chair as his hand involuntarily smoothed over the stubble on his strong jawline.

"Jessica, I don't want to be this person who is scaring you into doing something, but I'm thinking of how much you will regret it if you don't. He loves you. The last thing he wants is to find out you're going through all of this, and you never told him. And hopefully when you have this baby, and you are getting better, can you imagine how hard it will be for him to know you were going through all of that on your own? He won't just hate you; he will hate himself, and God forbid that poor child. Tell him because it will even be harder hearing it from someone else."

If Jessica had ever heard a threat, it was that, and it suddenly felt like the end of her world was balancing on it.

The pain tugging at her rib cage, along with the constant pounding at her chest, made her head ache. Her stomach churned as Mark stood and made his way towards the door. She knew he wouldn't tell Jake now. Not immediately. But the moment he turned his back and put his foot out of her office, she knew she was going to be constantly walking on eggshells around him, wondering when he was going to say something. The anxiety alone would kill her if the cancer didn't.

She needed to tell him. She knew it from the moment she saw her baby flicker on a monitor. With Mark now deciding to become a good Samaritan, it confirmed her decision even more so.

"I'll tell him." Her mouth opened reluctantly as the words fell like poison from her swollen, bitten lips.

"Good." Mark smiled softly.

Deep inside, she knew he wanted to help someone. That someone was not her, and if it was, it sure didn't feel like it.

"Just don't leave it too late, Jessica," he finished before leaving her office.

She knew what it meant: don't leave it too late because if she did, he would just jump right in there and do her dirty work for her.

Her blood felt like it was boiling in her veins. She wanted to smash something into tiny pieces.

Maybe Mark's head?

That sounded like a fantastic idea.

Two hours, a deep breathing session, cried out eyes, and a coffee or two later, Jessica scrambled her way out of the ball she had curled up into on her leather chair. Not the best place to relax, but it was the only option she had.

Placing her aching feet into her black stiletto heels, she grabbed her bag up from the floor and threw it over her shoulder.

She never knew her life's options could sprawl out in front of her in just one day.

This was going to kill Jake; she knew it. She hadn't even thought about what she was going to do if he told her to get rid of their baby.

Either way, he was going to hate her - for telling him and for not telling him. Realistically, she could never win this battle, no matter how hard she fought it.

She couldn't even see him today. To yell at him for telling everyone she was pregnant. Because she knew she would break down into a blubbering mess.

Why couldn't things be the way they were?

Today, she found herself thinking back on only six months ago, when she wasn't in a relationship with Jake, she wasn't pregnant, and she didn't have cancer. She could go out and have fun, be young, go clubbing with her friends when she liked, and she didn't have to answer to anyone for anything.

But for a strange reason, she felt lonely looking back. She didn't have anybody. Just herself and a messed up emotional state to keep her company.

"You ready?"

Her head shot up to a familiar voice and the face she recognized all too well standing at her doorway.

And there it was. Her question was answered. The reason she was so lonely six months ago. She didn't have Jake in her life. He was there. She just didn't have him. And as dark and as morbid as it may sound, cancer, or not, she wouldn't change it for the world. She loved him more than anything.

She always believed that everything happened for a reason.

Jake was her reason. But looking at him in that moment, she knew she was doing something she couldn't bear to think of. She was practically committing murder the longer she kept her mouth shut because, without his permission, or even his knowledge, she was killing him the same way the cancer was killing her.

"Yeah. I'm ready," she said, swallowing back the lump in her throat. "But I promised Michelle I would come and visit her this evening."

"Oh." He stuffed his hands in his pockets, trying to hide the disappointment in his voice.

"I'm also sorting some stuff out at the apartment, so I think it'll be better if I stay there tonight."

"Is everything okay, Jess? I mean, everything is all right with you?"

"Of course," she sighed, waving her hand casually, trying her best to place a believable smile on her lips.

Somehow, she doubted he believed her, and as he stepped further into her office, his eyes widened and lined creased his forehead in worry.

"Baby, have you been crying?"

"Oh." She pointed to the red and blotching patches surrounding her dark, water deep eyes. "This is embarrassing, but I'm reading a new book."

The deep chuckle that followed confirmed he believed every word. "You are so strange sometimes."

"Laugh it up," she said, shrugging her hands into the sleeves of her jacket and taking a few steps closer to him. He moved in to kiss her gently on the lips, and she tried her best not to melt right into him. "I really should get off." She shifted awkwardly, glancing at her wristwatch.

She wasn't lying about going to see Michelle, but she didn't need to sort out anything at her apartment. The only thing she was going to sort out at her apartment was her head. She needed to figure out the best way of telling him, and she couldn't do that if she stayed at his place.

"I guess I'll see you in the morning. If you need anything, just call." He nested his fingers in her hair. "I love you, sweetheart."

He kissed her one last time before turning to leave.

***

"That suits you." Michelle glanced towards Jessica, sitting on the comfort of the sofa with the baby held securely in her arms. "What is it with you?" Michelle wondered. "No offense, but you seem far too happy. You're making me depressed."

She *was* happy. She was so undeniably joyous, and she held onto that for the time she had with it. Ever so slowly, she was losing a grasp on the happiness.

And in one desperate attempt to hold a little tighter, she told Michelle about the baby, just to have the experience of telling someone without nerves or anxiety. She wanted to feel a moment of bliss one last time before she sat down with Jake.

"You're joking, right?" Michelle laughed, her eyes widening.

Jessica shook her head.

"Oh, shit." Michelle shot to her feet.

Jessica rocked the baby as Michelle's outburst put it through a brief uneasiness.

"Hush," Jessica giggled, holding her finger over her mouth.

"I can't believe it. I mean, how? Okay, don't answer that part. I didn't even know you were seeing someone. Who?" Michelle questioned giddily.

"Jake," she answered shyly, her cheeks burning red.

"Jake?" Michelle questioned, her eyes narrowing as she tried to gain any recollection of him. "You mean your brother's friend?"

That sounded wrong, and again the blood rushed to her cheeks.

"Oh, my God. I thought you two had this raging hatred towards each other?"

"It looks like I'm going to have to get used to him now. I have no other choice." She shrugged casually, still giggling at Michelle's reaction.

"I can't believe it." Michelle calmed as her eyes flashed a somber look. "I'm happy for you, Jess." She nodded before she stretched her body over to hug her friend briefly.

A few hours later, after the giddiness of baby talk and many cups of tea, Jessica only realized how late it was when her eyes began to get heavy.

"I better go. Some people have work to do around here," she teased, getting to her feet and letting the feeling of her blood rush through her legs like hot acid.

"Work? Ha. You will know exactly what proper work is like when the baby comes along."

Jessica hoped she would still be here.

***

Her apartment felt cold and lonely, so she went about doing her normal routine of switching on the lamps, television, and some heat before she took a hot shower and placed her tired body into blue silk pyjamas.

The last thing she was expecting as she sat down to watch a sappy soap was a loud banging on the door.

Didn't she make it clear to Jake that she would see him in the morning? Hadn't she told him she had things to sort out at the apartment?

Opening the door, her eyes almost rolled in her head. It wasn't the perfectly sculpted features of Jake that greeted her. Instead, her heart pounded viciously, threatening to make her collapse right there as dark raging eyes locked dead-on with hers.

"Rob? What are you doing here?" Her voice broke as the fear made her body freeze in place.

She didn't have to be a genius to figure out he wasn't there for a cup of coffee and weekly catch-up. She knew that look. It was the look that told every cell in her body to run in the opposite direction.

"You're pregnant," he growled. His hair was wild and falling into his face.

Christ. She thought Michelle would have had more sense than to tell her brother.

Her whole body jerked as he took a baby step closer. But it didn't matter how little the step was. He was still getting nearer to her. And with it came the undeniable smell of alcohol.

"You're drunk…"

"See," he cut her off, "My sister called me earlier to see how I was doing and accidentally let it slip that you had called for a visit. She also let slip that you were three months pregnant. She said I should be happy for you. You're finally moving on with your life. Can you believe she wanted me to do that? But I can't sit back and let you carry another man's child. The thing is Jessie! You might be finally *moving on*, but I haven't let you go yet. So, the moving on part is all in that little head of yours." He jabbed a finger into her temple.

"Rob, you're drunk, and you're scaring me, so right now I'm going to close this door, and we can talk about this in the morning when you are sober."

But she should have known better, and as she tried to close the door out, his fist sent it flying back and her entire body trembled in terror.

She felt trapped in the relationship again, with him backing her into a room and locking it behind him. He had her right where he wanted her until her body was going through so much fear, she couldn't phantom moving.

"No, Jess, you have it wrong." He stepped closer. "We are going to talk about it now," he demanded, before stepping inside and shutting the door behind him.

TWENTY-FOUR

Jessica stood still, staring into Rob's cold, black eyes. Her whole body went rigid, and her mind was betraying her and reliving the nightmarish scenes from her past. She remembered everything. She could almost smell the blood trickling down her pale cheeks, and the pain from the gash on her ribcage.

And here she was again, waiting for him to relish in her fear. Not even tears would come now. She was too scared, and she knew what was about to come. She ground her teeth, anxious, nervous, shaking, and with an overwhelming feeling of sorrow.

Was this it? Was she to just stand here and wait for him to damage every cell in her being, destroying any hope she had of protecting her baby?

"Rob, you're being stupid. Please," she begged, just about getting the words out of her mouth. "Calm down."

He laughed without any humour, an icy, disdainful laugh that left shivers creeping down her back.

"Jessie." He leaned towards her, using the name she hated so much; it slid from his lips like toxic. Every second, he was getting closer and closer. "You can't honestly expect me to calm down. I've just found out the love of my life is carrying someone else's child. I thought I already told you. I haven't given you permission to move on."

"Do you have some sort of memory loss, Rob? The last I can remember, I left you because you left a map of bruises all over my body. That was not love."

"I love you," he spluttered, appalled she might suggest otherwise. His eyes were stirring wildly now, and the fear in her body built until her hands were shaking uncontrollably. "How do you think it feels for me to find out from my sister that you are doing something you are supposed to be doing with me?"

"And what's that, Rob?" Jessica shot back.

"Starting a family."

"Rob," she said, her voice was softer now.

The last thing she wanted to do was provoke him. Shouting back at him wasn't going to help.

"When I met you in the coffee shop a couple of months ago, you said you changed, and I believed you. You seemed like you wanted me to be happy, and Lord knows I want it for you. But with somebody else. If you really loved me, you would let me go and allow me to be happy."

"So, this guy? Does he make you happy?" he suddenly asked, totally ignoring her previous suggestion.

Her nose wrinkled, and her eyes creased painfully as he crossed his arms over his chest. He seemed to calm a little. But talking about how Jake made her happy wouldn't keep his temper at bay.

"Do you really think this is necessary?" Jessica questioned, looking away for a moment.

"I don't. I should know who the guy is first, don't you think?"

Christ, hadn't Michelle mentioned who she was with? He was going to kill her. Jake and Rob hated each other long before Jake knew how he abused her. Rob used to say he didn't appreciate the looks he would get from Jake. Now Jessica knew that not only was Rob paranoid, but Jake knew something she didn't, he just couldn't put his finger on it. They despised each other, and if she told Rob who the father of this baby was, then he was going to flip the switch in his head and once again become the monster.

"Did I not ask you a question?"

All she could do now was stare up at him, feeling so helpless that it felt like the blood in her veins had turned to water. Her tears began to fall, and she didn't even attempt to stop them.

"You don't know him. Please just leave," she sobbed, the endless tears soaking her cheeks.

But he didn't leave. Instead, he grabbed her wrist and pulled her closer to him, the blood pulsing beneath her skin as his grip became tighter and her wrist twisted painfully.

"Rob," she tried to scream, but her voice was trapped in her throat.

"Who is it?" he demanded.

The silence was louder than anything she had ever heard.

"Who is it?" he screamed again, his hand like a bolt around her wrist.

"Jake," she whispered, knowing that after she said his name, Rob was going to go off the rails.

All she could do was hope and pray that someone was going to knock on the door and let her escape from this hell.

"Jake?" he trailed off, the deep hum of his laugh booming throughout her apartment. "Jake," he shrilled again, his mouth settling into a hard line. "You slut!" he cursed, grabbing the vase of flowers on the hallway table and smashing it to a thousand pieces against the wooden floor.

She tried to scream. She tried so hard. She opened her mouth and begged for a sound to come out, but all she felt was a burning in the back of her throat. Shock and fear had taken control of her body. The only instinct she had was to run, but she had nowhere to go. He was blocking the front door and her apartment was three flights up.

"Well." He tilted his head to the side and stared with that icy gaze that she always feared so much. "You can't expect me to love you when you have a part of him growing inside you."

"Oh, God," Jessica gasped.

She knew it wasn't a cue for him to leave. Protectively, her hand shot to her stomach. He couldn't harm her child. She wouldn't let that happen.

"Rob," she said soothingly, taking a step towards him. Being nice to him was her last resort. She had to do something.

But it didn't work. It never worked. She always tried and failed. Then tried and failed again.

But it never worked.

Goddammit, why did it never work?

He always won.

With a forceful grip around her shoulders, he backed her violently against the wall. The pain soared through her flesh until her head spun due to the impact.

"Rob, please. I am begging you. This baby," she stuttered.

Her head was pounding, and the room was spinning. But she needed to convince him that this baby's life was worth saving.

"This baby has nothing to do with Jake. It's mine. It's a part of me and if you hurt this baby, you are hurting me too."

Her sobs were coming thick and fast as she struggled to catch her breath.

He paced back and forth, running his fingers through his wild hair. Then he stopped, and she could feel his warm breath on her face. The smell of alcohol and stale cigarettes made her want to heave.

"I'm sorry about that, but it's nothing compared to the way you've hurt me."

And then it came.

Like all the times before.

The crushing fist moulded against her jawbone. The impact made her spin. Only for her hands plastered against the wall she would have slumped to the ground.

But in her heart, deep down, she knew this was only the beginning. He had no intentions of stopping there.

And she was right because just as she turned and tried to find some strength in her weak limbs, a gut-wrenching blow to the stomach knocked her to the floor.

Her body slumped against the wall, struggling for oxygen, and no matter how hard she tried to protect her belly with her arms, she still felt the pain.

Then he kicked and kicked, and then he kicked again.

She taught herself not to scream when he kicked. It only made things worse.

She tried to fight him off, but it didn't work.

It never did.

His shouting and ranting faded away into the distance, and the sight of her apartment blurred and spun around.

It did all of this until the pain began to disappear and lull dimly in the black.

Then all she saw was darkness.

TWENTY-FIVE

Beep… Beep… Beep… Beep… Beep

The darkness was turning into a grey area now—a grey area with an annoying, even beeping noise. She tried to force her eyelids open, but they wouldn't obey, and damn it, her head ached. She tried to shift her position, but as she did, an unforgiving pain shot through her body, and though she wanted to scream, only a moan escaped her.

"Jessica? Baby?"

That voice is familiar, she thought as a warm hand gripped hers.

"Chris, get the doctor. She's waking up," the high-pitched voice demanded.

And Chris? She knew him too, right?

"It's okay, sweetheart. You're going to be just fine. Can you hear me, Jessica?"

She tried to open her eyes to the sound of the voice, but once again, they failed her.

"Could you step back for a moment?" another deep voice interrupted, taking command of the situation.

Her heart was racing in her struggle to open her eyes. She could hear everything perfectly, so why could she not see what was going on?

"Jessica, this is Doctor Harris."

He took her hand.

"Just squeeze my hand if you can hear me."

She did as she was told.

"That's good, but I need you to stop struggling and take a deep breath."

"Why don't you talk to her?" Jessica heard the woman's voice again. "She might open her eyes for you, Jake?"

Jake?

Jake was here.

Her heart stopped as the doctor's hand was replaced by his. And without seeing him, she knew it was his touch. The familiar tingle spread across her palm.

"I need you to open your eyes, Jess."

Didn't he understand? She couldn't. She was trying her hardest.

"Baby," he whispered in her ear, and his breath swarmed across her neck. "I love you, and I need you to open your eyes for me. I need to see those beautiful sparkling blue eyes."

But she couldn't.

Instead, she gripped his hand tighter and drifted back into the darkness.

***

His fist came flying towards her, and he gripped her so tight she thought she was going to collapse. Then the pain shot through her body like fire.

"Stop!" she screamed, struggling against herself and the bedsheets.

Her eyes shot open and cold sweat streamed down her back.

She remembered.

She remembered everything until the pain in her heart hurt so much, her cheeks were drenched with salty tears.

"Jess. Breathe, baby. Breathe." Her eyes focused on the man lurking over her. "It's all right, sweetheart. I'm here. You're safe."

Jake.

That man was Jake, and she was safe.

But she couldn't say anything. The sobs had taken complete control of her body.

"The baby?" She panicked, placing her hands over her small bump. It was still there. But was the baby?

"The baby is fine," Jake assured her, looking away from her tear-filled gaze.

Her baby was okay. More moisture fell from her blotchy and swollen eyes with relief, but somehow Jake wasn't as excited as she was. An uneasy feeling settled in her stomach. She chose to ignore it and not question him about it.

"How long was I out?" she finally asked, her voice sounding hoarse and strained.

"Three days," he answered shortly.

"Three days?"

"You had me scared for a while. Good thing Michelle called me. It's not even worth thinking about—what could have happened if I didn't get there?"

"Michelle called you?"

"She was worried after she ended a call with Rob, so she called the office, and they gave her my number," he explained, rubbing his thumb against the back of her hand. "Watching you lying there was unbearable."

"Thank you," she whispered, swallowing the lump threatening more tears.

As her eyes focused more on his face, she noticed a deep gash under his brow, his knuckles cut and swollen.

"Did he do that?" She sat up and laced her fingers over the wound.

"Don't worry about it." He removed her hand.

He didn't have to say it. She already knew Rob came out the worse of the two.

"I'm going to tell the doctor you're awake. I'm sure he wants to examine you."

"Jake," she called after him.

She didn't want to be alone. She needed him. She wanted to feel the warmth of him close to her.

"I'll be right back. I promise," he said before leaning over to kiss her softly on her forehead.

A few moments later and Doctor Harris entered the room with a warm smile. But he was alone.

"Where's Jake?" she queried, hoping he was going to walk through the door after the doctor.

"I asked him to give us a few moments alone. He went for a short walk. The baby is doing fine," he started. "Jake got there just in time to save you both."

"I need to see him." She tried to sit up, the same uneasiness tying painful knots in her chest.

"Please, Jessica. Relax. Jake needs some time to digest things. There's been a lot for him to take in."

The silence that followed told her it wasn't only about what happened with Rob. He wouldn't look at her straight in the eyes, and that told her everything she needed to know.

"You told him, didn't you?"

Her heart sank.

Jake couldn't know.

"I'm sorry. I had to tell him."

"No. You didn't." Her voice was rising now, and the pounding was beginning at her temples.

"I did," Doctor Harris pressed. "You came in here so badly injured, I didn't know if I was going to have to operate on you or not, and the father of your child had a right to know if I was going to terminate the pregnancy."

She winced as her tears stung the deep cut across her jaw.

"Thankfully, you didn't need surgery," he went on. "And I can't terminate this pregnancy now. You're far too weak. Not only would you be too weak physically, but mentally and emotionally, you're nowhere near ready for any of that, and as your doctor, I can't recommend it."

She didn't care what he could recommend and what he couldn't. Jake knew about her cancer, and that was all that mattered. It explained why he seemed so distant earlier. She couldn't bear to think of him finding out like that.

She should have told him, but she was stupid and selfish, and it was obviously too late for that now.

"Could you tell him I would like to speak to him?"

"Of course." Doctor Harris nodded his head before leaving the room.

It was two hours before a dark shadow caught her eye, leaning against the door frame in the dull room. Her heart skipped a couple beats from just the sight of him—his strong arms crossed, his shoulders broad.

"Hey." She swallowed before biting down on her lip nervously.

He looked away from her. "Hi."

"Are you just going to stand there, or are you going to come in?"

"I can't, Jess." He nodded frantically before rubbing his fingers over his tired eyes.

It poisoned her to see him like that and to know that she had caused his heartache.

"I can't stand here and watch you wither away. I love you too much. I never thought I could love you so much and hate you for what you're doing to yourself. For allowing this to happen. For not coming to me. Christ, Jess, I would have been by your side every second and wore a smile doing it, because it was for you. Anything to keep you a second longer."

She was right from the beginning. There was no doubting how he would feel towards her when he found out.

There was silence between them then, neither able to find the right words. And she had to stew in this and witness the consequences of her actions play out.

"Now would be the time to say something," he prompted.

"I told you that you'd hate me."

His dark eyes widened for a moment, and she could almost see the memory replaying in his eyes.

"I thought you meant for being pregnant. Not for dying," he stated bitterly, and she flinched as his words hit her like another kick.

"I'm so sorry." She broke down. "I know I must seem like the most selfish person to you right now, but I couldn't get rid of our baby. Do you honestly think this is how I wished my life would plan out? For months, we were just having fun, there was no *us*, but then we became *us*, and everything changed. And I loved you like I never knew it was possible to love someone, and I have loved you more every day since. This is our baby and when I found out that you wanted a child, all I wanted was to make you happy. I'm not blaming you, because this mess is my fault. But I wanted to be a mother, Jake. And getting rid of this baby—our baby—was like letting this illness win. I'm never going to get another chance. I wanted to give birth, and I wanted it to be you by my side for it all. I swear I was going to tell you, and I'm so sorry that you found out this way."

Fresh tears brimmed in her eyes.

"I wanted our baby," he agreed confidently, exhaling loudly at her doubt, shifting from one foot to another, and crossing his arms again over his chest. "But not in exchange for your life, Jess."

She could see the reflection of his tears as his anger and frustration boiled over.

"Can't you see? I can't live in this world if you are not in it with me. I can't do it. I never could. I can't sit back and watch that baby kill you. I'm sorry. I can't look at that baby and know what it did. I love you so much, and it's unbearable to think of life without you, but I can't love something that I know it taking you away from me."

"You can't be saying you're giving up on our child. I'm not stupid. I know you love this baby," she shot.

He should be angry at her, not their unborn child.

"Deep down, I'll always love that child because it's a part of you. But I can't if it's taking you away from me. I'm sorry, Jess, but I wish you felt you could confide in me. If you did, you would have told me when you first found out you were sick."

"Nobody said I was going anywhere."

He swallowed hard before standing straight and striding swiftly towards her. Before she could take another breath, his lips covered hers in a heated kiss, his fingers tangling in her soft curls. She was falling into him willingly and without any doubt of her love for him. But every second that his lips lingered on hers, she could feel him go, losing his grip on her.

Slowly, almost painfully, he pulled away before wiping the tears from her cheeks.

"I'm so sorry," he whispered.

Then he turned on his heels, looking back only once through the eyes of a broken man.

He shattered her, but it wasn't anything less than she deserved.

TWENTY-SIX

2 months later…

"Hey, honey." Jessica's mother entered the room as she carefully removed her clothes from the wardrobe and packed her bulky bag. The dark circles around her mother's eyes looked too heavy for her petite, heart-shaped face.

She did this to her. If she had just told them from day one, none of this would have happened.

"Hey, Mom."

She tried to smile the sorrow away from her face, but her mother knew her better than that.

"Are you all set to go home?"

"I'm ready," Jessica let out, wincing from the pain of the fading bruises as she lifted her arms to tie back her hair.

"I'm going to miss you from around here, sweetheart. It was nice having you home again." Rose added.

Her parents convinced her it was best if she stayed with them until she got a little better. She lived out of home for so long, it didn't feel right. Or maybe it was that she no longer considered it her home. There was a place that made her heart leap when she thought of home, but with that jolt of happiness came endless tears.

The pain she felt physically was nothing compared to the emptiness. For a while, she felt numb to everything, and in a sick way, she wanted to stay in that state. She didn't want to feel the pain and the impact of

Jake walking away, but it was all she could think about.

The image of him turning on his heels haunted her since the day he said goodbye. It felt so final.

The pain eventually came. When it did, it hit her like a wave of fire, burning until there was nothing left but ash. There's was no rising from the rubble. Not this time.

She hadn't seen him since, and she couldn't blame him. How could she?

Looking back on the past couple of months, she didn't know how she climbed into such a frame of mind to believe that the best thing to do was keep it from him.

Was she possessed?

She thought she was protecting him, but in the end, she realized, the only person she was protecting was herself.

Her parents refused to come to terms with her illness, even though her doctor had told them there was a higher chance of survival than death.

But no matter the odds, they couldn't accept it.

They loved this baby as much as she did, but looking into their eyes, she could see what she saw in Jake's the day he told her he couldn't do it.

And it killed her to look at them. It pained her to the deepest part of her chest.

"I'll tell your father to put your bags in the car." Her mother broke the silence of her daze.

"Thanks."

Her sister April stepped quietly into the room. Her long blonde hair flowed over her shoulders. She was tapping the phone against the palm of her hand.

"The police called again," she finally said, sighing outwardly as her eyes roamed over Jessica's face. "They wanted to speak to you."

"They've wanted to speak to me for the last six weeks. I spoke to them enough in the hospital. There is nothing more I can tell them."

Jessica was getting annoyed. They called every day. Did they not get the hint that she wanted to forget about what happened to her?

"I know, but the police are pressing charges and they just wanted to go over the details with you."

"He beat me half to death. Jesus Christ, how difficult is that to understand?"

She stopped herself. These emotional outbursts had become too frequent and aimed at the wrong people.

"But he did this to you, Jess. He needs to be punished," April pressed softly, glistening tears welling in her green eyes.

"No, April." Jessica shook her head, swallowing the lump in her throat. "I did this to me."

"Okay, you know what?" April flung the phone on the desk, the landing making a loud thud against the pine wood. "I won't stand here and watch you blame yourself for this. You've been doing it for two months, and it's not your fault. Jesus, you thought what you were doing was right, and nobody can judge you for it. Maybe it was wrong, but your intentions were good. And I see you worry about this baby, but it will have plenty of people to love it. One of those people will be you because you're not going anywhere. You're my big sister, and I have always looked up to you for being a fighter." Mascara-soaked tears slid down her blushed cheeks as she bit down on her lip to stop it from trembling. "You need to fight through this, Jess. You can't leave us. You can't leave me. I need my big sister."

Jessica's eyes stung as the heavy tears pooled. She wasn't expecting that at all. Least of all from April. But as she stood and watched her little sister, swamped in her loosely fitted sweatshirt, her sandy hair flowing around her narrow cheeks, and endless tears escaping from her hazel eyes, Jessica couldn't stop the sobs escaping.

"Oh, April. Come here." She stepped towards her, gesturing for her to come closer.

And she did. Without hesitation, she ran into Jessica's arms as if she were a child again.

"I'm going to fight as hard as I can, okay?" Jessica promised, whispering against the top of her head.

April nodded, pulling away from the warmth of her embrace, and scrubbed her hands down her face to wipe away the tears.

"Don't worry about Jake. He'll come to his senses. He can't stop loving you overnight. That pain in the ass will never stop loving you, and even though you might not think it, he loves that baby. He won't stay away."

How wrong her little sister was?

He hated her.

But instead of disagreeing, she plastered a smile on her face and simply said, "I hope you're right, sis. I really do."

Forty minutes and tear-loads later, she arrived outside her apartment building with her father. Her mother decided it was best she stayed at home. Apparently, she had cleaning to do. Jessica knew what she was doing. She was distracting herself. She didn't want to see her daughter leave to live on her own. And with Jessica sick and pregnant, her mother wanted to take care of her. Who could blame her? If the roles were reversed, Jessica would want to do the same.

She placed her hand over her bump—still feeling the faint hint of a bruise on her skin.

It must have been an omen that she kept this place. She needed it more than ever. Two months ago, the only place she saw as a home was Jake's house.

It was scary how things changed.

Looking down the long hallway, memories flashed violently in her head, making her temples pound. She could imagine Rob storming through this hallway in a rage with thoughts of what he was going to do to her in his mind.

"Are you all right, sweetie?" her father asked.

She tilted her head to look at him, and to her surprise, she had stopped and was staring straight at the ground.

"You don't have to do this, you know? You could come home with me again."

"No." She shook her head. "I can do this. I'm fine." She smiled softly.

She pushed herself forward, forcing the terrifying thoughts to the back of her mind. She could do this without those images replaying in her head like a horror movie.

As she reached into her bag for her keys, the door swung open, sweeping a whoosh of air across her face.

"Welcome home," a voice squealed before popping her head out from behind the door.

"Oh." Jessica's eyes widened as Sharon's face came into view. "What the hell are you doing here?"

"What kind of friend would I be if I weren't here to greet you? And I cleaned around a bit. The place was getting dusty."

It was more like she was there to remove the remaining stains of blood from the floor, but Sharon didn't say that.

"Don't just stand there looking at me. Get your ass in the apartment. I wasn't slaving around here all day for nothing."

"Isn't it great to know that it came from the kindness of your heart? I knew you were being too soppy for a minute," Jessica teased as she strolled into the apartment, closing her eyes briefly as she strode swiftly past the hallway, deciding not to comment on the new rug. The old one must have been soaked in blood.

The place was almost sparkling. The fresh smell of lemon and bleach was refreshing as it burst through her senses, and the cool breeze blowing through the windows made her gold curtains fly in the air as if they were dancing together.

Her father kissed her gently on the cheek before wrapping her in his warm embrace. "I know you will be fine here with Sharon. I better be off."

"Thank you, Dad." She pulled away, smiling up at the tired face of her father. This had taken its toll on him. He was just too proud to admit it.

"Never hesitate to call us if you need anything. You know where we are, and I'm sure your mother will call around more often to check up on you," he said.

"I'm sure." She smiled before seeing him out.

Sharon's greedy hands were all over her bump the moment she shut the door. "Wow, Jess. That baby is getting big."

"You're telling me. I'm the one who has to carry this thing around."

"It will all be worth it, though. I can spoil your baby now because I am never pushing a child out through my—"

"Okay. I get the idea." Jessica stopped her before she had the chance to share the graphical details.

"Go sit down. I was about to make some tea."

Jessica did as she was told.

A few moments later, Sharon handed her a steaming cup of strong tea. The hot liquid glided down her throat and instantly made her feel more relaxed, more at home.

"Still no word from Jake, then?" Sharon sighed, taking a large gulp as she positioned herself on the sofa, throwing her legs up after her.

"No." Jessica's chest tightened. "I think he would prefer if I disappeared off the face of the Earth."

"No, he wouldn't. He's hurt. He still loves you. He can't stop it, even if he fights it. But he still worries about you and the baby."

Her eyes narrowed.

Sharon looked guilty as sin.

"How do you know that?"

Her eyes roamed everywhere but on Jessica as she quietly said, "Because he still calls me every day to see how you're doing."

She almost set her throat on fire as she choked on the hot tea. That was a sizeable chunk of information Sharon had failed to tell her.

"Did that somehow slip your mind? Did you fall and hit your head and, whoops, *a-big-thing-I-need-to-tell-my-friend* fell out" Jessica blurted, her eyes wide.

Sharon's lips turned down, rearing back. "Did you hit your head and, whoops, *I-have-cancer* fell out," she shot back.

"Touché."

They both smiled.

"He didn't want me to tell you. He's hurting Jess. We all are. And you might be dying. I can't even get over that, so I can't imagine how Jake feels. You're carrying his child, remember? Give him time. That's all he needs."

"Does he really call you every day?"

She cried herself to sleep every night because she hadn't even heard his name since the hospital and now, she comes home to find out he has been contacting her best friend to see how she was.

"Every day since you came home from the hospital." She shrugged, placing her black, bob-cut hair behind her ears.

"I hate to make things worse for him, but I'm going back to work tomorrow. I already told Mr. Johnson."

"I'm sorry." Sharon poked her. "You're not going back to work tomorrow. I'm not worried about Jake's sorry ass. I'm worried about you. You can't go back to work. You're not ready."

"I am ready, and I'm going back to work tomorrow. I have nothing else to do, and it will bore me sitting at home by myself," Jessica moaned, pinching the bridge of her nose.

"But you won't be by yourself. I'll be here."

She wasn't serious, was she?

No, no, no.

That was not happening.

"What do you mean? You will be here?" Jessica asked, scepticism in her tone.

"I'm going to stay here with you for a while. You need somebody around."

"I'm going to stop you right there." Jessica waved her hand in dismissal. "You are not staying here with me. I love you, and I am extremely grateful to you, but I would kill you if I had to live with you. I'm perfectly fine here on my own. Rob won't come back."

Sharon clicked her tongue against the roof of her mouth, frustration burning in her eyes.

"How do you know that?"

"I don't," Jessica answered honestly, shrugging her frail shoulders. Then she realized how stupid she was sounding. "Okay, you can stay here with me for a few days, but that's it. I swear I will kick your skinny ass out of this apartment if you don't leave when I tell you to," Jessica warned, trying her best to keep the smirk from her lips.

"Fine. A few days." Sharon gave in, grunting loudly. "Anyway." Sharon rolled her light grey eyes. "It looks like I won't be able to stop you from going to work, so if you're wondering, your clothes are in the closets. I went and got them from Jake's."

She nodded.

What else could she do?

It was her own damn fault.

Typical.

Everything was going perfectly, and she had to ruin it.

Why didn't she just open her stupid, idiotic mouth in the first place? None of this would have happened.

With all of that still firmly floating around her mind, Jessica went to bed early.

And she slept.

For the first time in a long time, she closed her eyes and welcomed sleep.

So as the alarm buzzed on her bedside desk, she rolled over and hit it so hard she could have sworn she fractured something in her hand.

"Good morning," a voice mumbled from the other side of the bed.

"Jesus Christ, Sharon." She gasped, holding her hand over her heart. "But good morning."

The worst thing about having a one-bedroom apartment?

She had to sleep with her best friend and live with her.

Throwing the covers back, she shivered as the frosty morning air swept at her feet.

In the bathroom mirror, she sighed at her reflection. She'd lost weight and even with a good night's sleep, the dark bags under her eyes were a sure sign of exhaustion and stress.

As she pressed her hands against the sink, she noticed her collarbone was more prominent than before and her face had become drawn.

It wasn't a shock that Sharon was still sprawled out on the bed when she returned.

"Sharon," she raised her voice a little. "Get your ass out of my bed. Now. You're going to be late for work."

"I'm up." She yawned.

As Sharon was in the shower, Jessica dried her hair and let the natural curls fall down her back before applying some foundation, blush, and mascara. Rummaging through her closet, she picked out a black wrap dress. Her choice of clothing that both fit and looked professional had become limited. Even though her bump was still small, none of her shirts would close around it.

"Sharon, I'll see you later," she called into the bedroom before slipping her arms into her red wool coat and stuffing her keys into her handbag. "Love you."

"Uh-huh. Love you too," was the only response she received as she watched Sharon tumble around the bedroom, trying her best to get her legs into her trousers.

Jessica strolled towards her car, smiling and waving to the neighbours that passed. She tried to block out their pitiful glares. They heard what happened. She had a few nosy neighbours—the ones that sit at home all day and have nothing better to do but stick their noses in other people's business and feed their cats. They were the ones who would start asking questions when Jessica was no longer around.

Her leg bounced as she stopped at the traffic lights before the turn to her office building. Her stomach cramped with unexpected butterflies. She heard that when the baby moves it feels like butterflies, but this wasn't the baby moving.

Could she face him? Could she just ponder around the office, knowing that the father of her child was upstairs and wanted nothing to do with them?

"Oh, God." Her hands shook as she pressured them against the wheel, her knuckles turning white. "What the hell am I doing?"

The loud honk of the car behind knocked her out of her trance and she quickly put her leg on the accelerator to turn the corner and into an empty parking space.

She already prepared herself for the sympathetic looks she would get from her co-workers. She wasn't sure if Jake had told people about her illness. She assumed they all knew about the attack.

As she walked out of the elevator and onto the soft carpet, the bright smiling face of her junior secretary came flying towards her with her arms opened wide, ready to pull her into an embrace.

"It's so good to have you back. Your replacement was a complete bitch," Sophie grunted, going on an immediate rant as she flicked her flaming red hair onto her back.

"It's good to be back." Jessica smiled, grateful for the warm welcome. "And you seemed to have survived with me gone. The replacement couldn't have been that much of a bitch."

"I had to stop myself from swinging her out the window by the legs too many times. Believe me when I say I'm more than relieved to have you back."

"Thank you."

"But you should have waited until tomorrow. Mr. Johnson has scheduled one of those monthly staff meetings for twelve this afternoon."

Wasn't that fantastic?

She hated those meetings.

And Jake was going to be there. She wouldn't be capable of keeping her roaming eyes from him. Why couldn't someone come along, shake her, and tell her it was all a bad dream?

But she created this nightmare. She was the only one that could wake herself. It felt like one of those dreams where you were falling and the ground was getting closer and closer, but you never hit it.

Don't they say if you hit the ground, you never wake up? Jessica had simply hit every bump on the way down.

"We heard what happened to you? You know this place. News spreads fast." She threw her eyes up. "Jake gave me some basic details. I'm sure he didn't want to have your business talked about. He only told me because I asked."

Her body froze. She prepared herself for the sympathetic stares, but no amount of preparation was good enough for the real thing.

"Your ex is such a jerk to do that to you," Sophie snapped. It filled her eyes with sheer rage.

Jessica relaxed a little then, and her shoulders collapsed as the tension dripped from her body. Maybe he didn't tell them about the cancer after all.

"Yeah, he is," Jessica breathed.

"But you're good now, right?"

"Of course," Jessica agreed. "I better be off. I have a lot of catching up to do?"

"See you later." Sophie waved before slipping in behind the tall desk to carry on with her work.

As Jessica settled back into her office, something suddenly hit her. Did Jake even tell them they had broken up? Sophie would have surely said something if he did, right?

He must have said something. He was hardly going around answering questions about her, letting people think they were still together.

That was a stupid thought.

Sophie didn't want to be nosy.

That must be it.

After three hours of solid work, it was time to face the dreaded meeting.

Forcing the bravest face she could muster, she took her belongings and headed upstairs to the conference room. She was a little early so there wasn't many people to stare at her, but soon the large oval table became surrounded by her colleagues. They didn't ask questions. They just gave a brief hello and a strange look.

"Welcome back," Mark whispered as he took a seat to her right.

"Thanks." She smiled, turning to look at him.

"She's back," a deep, loud voice boomed throughout the large room.

Jessica turned to see Mr. Johnson stepping towards her in even strides. "Our very talented, very beautiful…" He stepped closer and his wrinkled eyes narrowed, his gaze dancing from her face to her belly and back again. "Very pregnant Jessica is back to us. Welcome back. You were sorely missed," he told her.

Mr. Johnson turned and her eyes shot to the door, where the man standing there made her heart skip a beat and her breath catch in her throat.

"Jake, you made it." Mr. Johnson acknowledged him with a dip of his chin.

Jake stood, frozen, looking at her with an unrecognizable stare. His face was a look of severe pain. His dark eyes searched her face. His hair was still short, but slightly longer than it was when she last saw him. He too had also lost weight, she noted. It was a look that made her heart ache.

"Take a seat next to your beautiful girlfriend. You must be so happy she's back." Mr. Johnson gestured towards the seat next to Jessica. It was the only one free.

Hold on.

Did he say Jake's *girlfriend*?

"You two always were the office lovebirds, even when you argued." Mr. Johnson sighed, staring at them. The entire table let out a hushed laugh in unison.

Jessica reminded herself she needed oxygen as Jake took a seat beside her. Her whole body trembled as he pressed against her, the smell of his cologne eroticizing her senses.

But she was confused.

She was about to object to her boss's statement when Jake's hand came down on her thigh, making her suck the words back in.

"Shut up, Jess," Jake warned, leaning over so she was the only one to hear.

Her entire face tensed.

What was he talking about?

And the more she relaxed into her seat, the more she realized what was happening. His stare was seeping through her, making her blood so hot she was heaving in tiny gasps. All she wanted to do was reach out and touch him.

His eyes roamed from her face to the small bump and back again.

"You haven't told anybody?"

He looked away then to make sure nobody was paying attention to their intimate conversation.

"I'm getting there," he confessed. "I never realized it would be so hard to let you go. And seeing you again, I'm asking myself if I can?"

TWENTY-SEVEN

As the meeting ended, Jessica gathered her belongings in a *hurry-and-get-the-hell-out-of-there* fashion. She couldn't bear to be there. She couldn't look at him and know she caused the pain written in his deep-set eyes. It was crushing to feel him close to her, to feel the heat of his body and know she had caused his hate.

She wasn't going to lie. Her heart made an instant tremble and her knees turned to jelly when he said he wasn't sure if he could give her up. But he hadn't looked at her since, and even as he said the words, it was like a chisel scraping against ice. She needed to walk away; in fear, she was going to cause him any more hurt than his big heart was already struggling with.

Opening the door to her office, a firm grip pulled at her wrist, tugging at her desperately, until she spun around and locked with his wild eyes. His breathing was coming in thick, heavy pants, and Jessica noticed something she hadn't noticed in the meeting. Along with the dark stubble on his cheeks came the undeniable scent of stale liquor.

"You can't just run away like that," he told her, before dragging her into her office and shutting the door behind him.

"Have you been drinking?" she asked, already knowing he was going to give her a smart answer. She was prepared for it.

"I apologize if it offends you, but I found out recently that the woman I love is killing herself."

Jessica let out a long, quiet breath.

She deserved that.

"I'm allowed to drink myself senseless at night when all I can do is think about you and what you're doing to yourself." He paced back and forth, running a frustrated hand through his hair, and loosening the knot in his tie.

Her office was dull. The dark clouds outside threatened heavy rain and thunder. It may have been the beginning of summer, but the weather reflected the mood between them both.

"Jake, the whole drinking thing, it's not who you are. Please stop," she begged.

"And you suddenly know who I am now, do you? Don't worry your little self about me. It didn't seem to bother you the past few months," he spat, staring straight at her.

It felt like a thousand knives soared from him and pinched right at her flesh, tightening the air around her lungs until her throat closed in. She flinched, and by the way the warm colour in his eyes suddenly flickered, he knew he hurt her. But any regret he briefly felt disappeared when his cool guard came flying back up again.

She didn't fight back. She fought against him for too long now. Instead, she stayed silent and let his words seep through her like a deadly punishment. She deserved everything he was going to throw at her.

"Don't worry, Jessica. I don't drink on the job. As you can probably tell—now that you know me so well—I'm perfectly sober."

And he was. There was nothing glossy or foggy about his eyes. And she knew when he was drunk. Right now, he was just downright mad.

"Tell me something." He stepped closer to her. "Did you enjoy telling me how much you loved me, knowing you were dying? You must have been laughing inside the entire time."

"Don't be so ridiculous, Jake? Can you hear yourself at all?"

"I can hear myself fine," he snarled. "Goddamn it, I love you. I love you so much it hurts. It hurts like hell. But I can't love that thing." He pointed towards her stomach. "Do you know what's worse? Knowing that I helped create what is killing you. I mean—"

"Shut up, Jake," she screamed.

His eyes widened before he stuffed his hands into his pockets, waiting for what she was going to say next.

She had enough. Blaming her was one thing, but he had to stop blaming this on their baby.

"This child has nothing to do with what is going on. I was sick before any of this ever happened. I was sick before *you* happened. And I was doing fine, but you *did* happen. I couldn't stop it. And even if I could, I wouldn't. What? You don't think I love you as much as you love me? Sometimes, I worry I love you too much. But I'm sick, Jake. With or without this baby, I am sick. And yes, I did the most stupid thing ever, and I never told you. I was selfish to think you would accept this baby whether I lived or died."

He winced at those words. She hadn't even dealt with it herself yet.

"But I couldn't give it up. I got greedy in thinking I could have you both when I obviously can't," she confessed, swallowing the growing lump in her throat. Not that it helped. The tears still fell from her eyes.

His expression seemed to soften then, his lips parting as he roughly ran his hands over his face.

"But why didn't you get rid of it, Jessica? We could have tried. There are plenty of other options out there."

She couldn't answer him. She was completely numb.

"I'm not stupid. I know what you're like. You would have told me if something wasn't scaring you so much."

There was nothing but silence between them, and she knew it wasn't a good enough response.

"For Christ's sake, Jess. Tell me why you did it?"

"Because I had a baby taken away from me before," she blurted before breaking down into an uncontrollable torrent of heart-wrenching sobs.

On sheer instinct, he glided two steps towards her and rested his hands on her arms to stop her from shaking, seating her in the leather chair behind them. Kneeling, he removed a loose curl from sticking to her wet cheeks.

"What are you talking about?"

She tilted her head so that her eyes were level with his and moistened her lips before nervously biting down on them. She already said that much. She needed to explain. No more holding back. No more secrets.

"I don't need to tell you about what Rob did to me," she breathed. "But four months before we broke up, I found out I was pregnant."

She felt Jake's heavy breath across her face, but he didn't react, and she was grateful. She lowered her head and fumbled with a loose thread on her blouse.

"It was supposed to change things. He was great when we first found out. And I was getting what I always wanted. I was going to be a mother. He promised me everything would be different. I probably should have known." She shrugged helplessly. "But one night I came home, and he flipped. I was the only thing in sight he could pick his mood out on. I lost the baby. So, when I found out I was pregnant this time, I knew if I told you I was sick, you would choose my life over the baby. And I couldn't let another man take that away from me, Jake.

"I suppose what really made my decision final was that it was yours. I loved you too much. Maybe I thought I would get back what he had taken away from me."

She didn't dare look at him. She was petrified of what she'd see. Truthfully, all she wanted to do was fall into his arms and for him to tell her that everything was going to be okay. That they could get through this together.

"I should have killed the bastard when I had the chance. Why didn't you tell me?"

"I told nobody until now. As you've probably already guessed, I'm surprisingly good at keeping things to myself." A smile edged at the corner of his mouth in her best attempts to lighten the dark mood between them.

"Look." She threw her hands in the air. "I'm truly sorry. I will tell you forever how sorry I am, and it won't be enough. I love you. Nothing in this world could make me hate you. I did this to protect the people I love most, but it turns out I end up hurting them even more by keeping things from them. I did all of this to avoid the way you're looking at me, and I'm sorry," she said, standing, and backing away to put space between them.

She needed air, and fast. Her office was beginning to spin. She turned to face him one last time.

"I did this to you, so I can't expect you to accept this baby, and now I know why you can't. It's not your fault if you can't love—"

"I lied," he let out, taking a lung full of air.

"What?"

"I was mad. I was mad at everyone. I was angry at you, at Rob, at the doctors, but the only person I could tell myself was the real problem was the baby, when I really wanted to be mad at you. I couldn't be mad at any of you. I was trying to make it go away by blaming someone. But deep down, I realized, it wasn't anyone's fault.

Jess, I couldn't stop loving you and that baby if I tried."

She was dreaming, wasn't she? This was the part where someone woke her, right?

"Jess, I love you. I love this baby. And as much as I refuse to let something happen to you—either way—I'll be here for our child, no matter what. I can't believe I was idiotic enough to make you believe I wouldn't."

Nobody was waking her, and her heart was about to explode. She placed her palm against the door to steady herself. The only thing reminding her that this was real was the hot tears flowing down her cheeks.

She couldn't speak. She couldn't feel. She couldn't even think.

"Goddamn it, woman, say something," he demanded.

She tried to part her lips and let the words flow, but they got stuck in her throat somewhere.

Was he saying he forgave her or was she having a serious dose of her own imagination?

"If you're not going to say anything, I'm going to have to take advantage of your silence."

He stepped towards her. He was so close now she could feel his breath on her face. He lowered his mouth to hers, and every muscle in her body was going lax. It wasn't demanding. It wasn't urgent. It was devastating. The kiss tumbled her deeper and deeper, bombarding her with emotions she had no defence against. His feelings were free and ripe and poured over her, into her, so that she was covered, filled, and surrounded by them.

"I love you," he breathed as he brushed his fingers through the strands of her hair.

The kiss crushed her, and there was no going back after that. She had never been kissed like that—even by Jake.

"If I'm dreaming, please don't wake me," she pleaded, feeling fresh tears brimming in her eyes.

He chuckled quietly, deep in his throat.

"Baby, this isn't a dream," he assured before kissing her to near death.

TWENTY-EIGHT

It was amazing how effortless life could suddenly be; sucking the most vulnerable into every inch of its perfection until they realize too late it brought them up just to let them fall. But Jessica refused to think of that now. She wasn't going anywhere tonight or the nights to follow. She was going to stay right where she belonged, in Jake's arms, in his house, in his heart, with their baby.

Something like that could never crush her. Something like that was truly effortless.

She smiled to herself, closing her tired eyes, and gently gliding her fingers over the growing bump as she listened to Jake make a racket with the cupboards in the kitchen downstairs. She sprawled across his enormous bed in sweatpants and one of his oversized t-shirts. She loved him with all her heart, but sometimes he was a complete pain in the ass.

"Jake, do the words *'be quiet'* mean anything to you?" she half shouted, half laughed, unable to stop herself as he let out an exasperated sigh.

It was easier to notice she was becoming weaker and weaker as the weeks went on. The dark circles under her eyes showed just how much pain she was in, even if she didn't admit it.

A week ago, she took maternity leave from work as she reached seven months. Not because she wanted to, but because Jake insisted. After all, he was the one who was with her when her legs weakened, her heart raced at erratic speeds, and her hands trembled as if she had just taken them out of ice water. It also didn't help that she was now carrying a baby who thought it was training for a rugby team.

They made an agreement with her doctors that they would bring her into the hospital at 34 weeks to conduct a caesarean section, deliver the baby, and perform a complete hysterectomy. They wanted to deliver the baby earlier, but she wanted them to guarantee her baby's survival. They couldn't do that. Instead, they gave her the infamous line, "we will try as hard as we can."

At least this time, when she made her sometimes insane decisions, Jake was right beside her to show his support. He loved this baby as much as she did, and he may have fussed and rambled about the fact that she was giving the doctors less time to take away her cancer, but he also knew where she was coming from, wanting to wait longer. He sucked it up, knowing she was as stubborn as a mule, and no matter what he said, she wouldn't change her mind.

Jessica couldn't stop the giggle bubbling in her throat as he dragged his feet lazily onto the carpet of their bedroom and threw himself onto the bed.

He was tired and stressed. She could see it in the slight puffiness under his eyes. Even so, there was still a certain flame in his glazed orbs. He glanced at her from the corner of his eye, revealing some honey specs dancing in a fiery aura. She crossed her arms, leaning them on her bump, grinning smugly to herself.

"Spit it out," she prompted. She could tell he needed to vent about something.

With a long breath, he frowned, pulling his eyes closer together so that the bridge of his nose wrinkled. It looked like he needed to sneeze. That made her laugh louder. But he said nothing. He glared. That wasn't helping. She could never take him seriously when he looked at her like that.

Another glare.

She bit down on the inside of her cheek to stop the next eruption of giggles.

You put your hand in a fire, you're going to get burned.

"You're off work a week, and you have our entire kitchen rearranged."

She tried not to laugh. She really did.

"I'm sorry, but had you noticed the state the cupboards were in.

Nothing was where it should have been. What were you looking for, anyway?"

He shook his head helplessly and rolled his eyes.

"I can't even remember anymore," he confessed, stuffing his head into the pillowcase.

He said something else after that. She was sure he was cursing her, but she couldn't make out his muffled sounds.

Jessica swayed, hitting her body against his playfully.

"Come on. We both know it's not the cupboards that are bothering you."

He lifted his head out of the pillow to stare at her, his expression serious but not serious enough for her to believe him.

"Jake, everything is going to be fine," she reassured him, touching the warmth of his skin, feathering her fingertips along his mouth.

"It won't. You're going to the hospital tomorrow to have this baby. It's not even about the baby. It's about what they are doing after the delivery."

"I knew it wasn't the cupboards." She smiled before kissing him softly. "Everything is going to be fine. Stop worrying."

"But what if—"

"Stop asking yourself what if," she demanded. It was breaking his heart when he thought about it like that, and she knew it.

"This time tomorrow night we are going to have a beautiful little baby to fuss over, no matter what the outcome is with me."

"The only outcome there will be is that I will take you home so we can raise our child together," he stated firmly, furrowing his brows in disbelief that she would even say something like that.

"I'm only preparing myself."

"Then stop."

"Jake," she pleaded, smoothing her fingers over her tired eyes. "We have been over this a thousand times. Can we not talk about it? We have a baby to look forward to." She begged.

"I'm sorry," he sighed.

Turning onto his back, he sat against the headboard, wrapping his arm around her shoulders to tuck her closer to him. "Have you thought of any names for our little girl yet?"

He changed his mind on the gender at some stage when multiple people told Jessica she was carrying high. Apparently, it was an old wives' tale to signal the birth of a baby girl.

"It's a boy." She shrugged, feeling like this conversation was a daily battle.

"It's a girl," he fought back.

"It's a boy."

"Girl."

"Does it really matter?" She patted his chest.

It didn't matter. Not to her. And they already converted one bedroom into a beautiful nursery, painted apple green and decorated with animal wall stickers. The sleigh cot took pride of place in the center of the room beneath a mobile with hanging stars.

"Of course not. I just miss how we used to always be at each other's throats."

"And here I am," she said sarcastically. "I went from killing you to being pregnant with your child. What were the chances?"

"The chances were pretty high. I was counting down the seconds until you threw yourself at me."

"You are so full of shit."

"I should have kept those panties you left here the first night we slept together. Just as a souvenir to show you I won in the end."

"You only won the battle."

"Crafty, Connors," he said, suddenly swooping over her.

She looked to him, her bump, and then back again.

"Not in front of the baby, Williams." She pouted, teasing him as she licked her lips, biting on the raw skin.

He smirked before lowering his head and devouring her with his hungry kiss.

TWENTY-NINE

"Mr. Williams?" a distant voice called his name, but he couldn't move. Memories of the previous night swarmed around in his head. Everything she said about preparing for the worst. How could he prepare for the worst? He couldn't lose her. Not now. Not when he had her for good.

He could hear her laugh fill his ears and surround him like a warm honey coating, pouring into him like liquid pleasure. He could even smell the sweet scent that clung to her body, no matter where she went. The smell of vanilla burst through his senses in a wild torrent, driving him crazy.

He needed her back with him. He needed to hold her.

They took her away forty minutes ago. He was pacing up and down in front of them ever since—eyes closed, fully dressed in a hospital gown. She looked so helpless, so lifeless—everything she shouldn't have been.

Her last words, of course, were ones that made him laugh.

"Keep your eyes away from the nurses," she warned before kissing him gently, telling him she loved him, and then drifting off into her own oblivion.

"Mr. Williams?" the voice pressed.

His body jerked as his name finally registered. He looked to see a nurse staring straight back at him, her crystal-like eyes scanning him like he was mad.

“I’m sorry,” he apologized, shaking his head.

“Would you like to come and see your son?” she asked, placing a gentle smile on her face.

His son.

Holy shit.

He had a son.

“I have a son?” he gasped, staring at her with googly eyes.

“Yes, you have a son.” She was obviously immune to these reactions from new fathers. “A whole 5lbs 6 ounces of a son. Great weight, considering he was born early.”

He couldn’t help but laugh. His body burned with adrenaline.

Jess was right. It was a boy. She would be so smug right now.

“I want to see him,” he finally answered, realizing he said nothing yet. “How is she?” His voice broke.

“She’s doing fine. Those doctors are miracle workers. It won’t be too long more, and they will be done in there.”

“Thank you.” He was grateful for her soft smile and the reassuring hand on his shoulder. “Just give me a minute. I need to tell her family.”

He practically sprinted to the waiting area where they were all seated, including Jess’s brother. He came home recently. Sharon, a person he’d never seen nervous, was curled up on the chair, biting her perfectly manicured nails.

A sea of awaiting faces stared at him, waiting for him to say something, anything but what they dreaded most. They stood, and he could almost hear the echo of their heartbeats.

“They’re still operating on Jess, but we have a boy,” he announced proudly, oddly surprised to feel a painful lump rising in his throat.

There was nothing but silence for a long moment until Sharon let out a painful scream.

“Oh. My. God. Oh. My. God,” she repeated hysterically. “She had a boy. She had a boy. And he’s alive,” she murmured the last part to herself.

A song of congratulations came flying at him, hugs and handshakes from everyone.

“You better get down there and see your son, my boy.” Chris patted his back, the smile of another proud father gracing his lips before they made their way through the bright wide halls, hearing every step as it clunked against the tiled floors.

The rest of them followed close behind. He met the nurse where he left her and took a mental note to get her name by the end of this.

She directed them to the neo-natal unit.

Machines hummed, small bodies, even smaller breaths… and hope. He didn't want to see his son hooked to machines. But while he was in there with people who cared, there was hope.

"There are only two allowed in at a time. Would you like to bring someone with you?"

He wanted to bring Jess with him. He wanted her to experience this. For her to hold their child and feel the sheer happiness.

He turned and faced her family. The choice he was going to make was obvious.

"April, do you want to come in with me?"

Her eyes lit up, endless tears streaming.

"Of course, I do." She smiled, taking a deep breath to calm her unstable nerves.

Jake had always seen her as a little sister, and right now, all he wanted to do was wrap her up like a child and hug her. She needed it as much as he did. So, he did. As she stepped towards him, he pulled her into his embrace, kissing the top of her head.

"Jess wouldn't want to see you like this. Take a deep breath. Everything is going to be absolutely fine, sweetheart," he assured her, placing an encouraging hand on her back.

The nurse guided them both into the warm, dimly lit room. His heart was pounding at an unnatural pace, resonating throughout his body.

He was about to see his son for the first time.

The nurse gestured to a small incubator.

Then it happened.

Jake never knew so much love could smack him right in the face the way it did when he looked at the small body, comfortably lying in this glass box with only a hole to put his hand through.

"Is Jake Williams crying?" April teased.

"I think I am," he sniffed, not ashamed of the overwhelming feelings brought on from looking at this tiny little boy.

That little boy was his son. His life. Something that he created with the woman he loved more than anything.

"He's so tiny," April squealed, cooing at her new nephew.

Jake reached in and placed his finger in his little boy's hand, careful not to touch the wires connected to him. He couldn't take his eyes off him. He smiled at every blink, every sound, every movement. Everything about him was so perfect.

"Sorry, Jake." April patted his back. "But I'm afraid he got his beauty from his mother."

"I don't have any problems with that." He sighed, taking everything in. "I've never seen anything so perfect."

He couldn't wait for Jess to see him. She was going to be a blubbering mess, and he was going to be there to laugh at her, never admitting that he also cried when he first saw their son.

"Got any names picked out yet?"

"Jess said one would come to her when she saw the baby."

It saddened him he couldn't hold his child, to feel him in his arms. Instead, he sat there and listened to the annoying, constant beeping that told him his little boy's heartbeat was stable.

It would be worth it, though, to have his child and Jess well again, and back in their home, where he could take care of them. He just wanted to be a father and make Jess happy.

He patted the outline of the square box hidden in his coat pocket.

Someday, he thought.

Someday, she was going to be his for life.

THIRTY

Jessica squinted as a light shone down on her. She closed them again, hoping that this wasn't the light she should go to. Heaven wasn't meant to be so painful.

She tried to moisten her dry lips by rolling her tongue over the skin, but her mouth felt like sandpaper.

It was then her ears adjusted to the sound of a constant, even beat. She flinched and cried out a quiet moan as she tried to position herself. Her frail hands trembled beneath her weight.

Opening her eyes again, she scanned the room. The white walls were carelessly decorated with tasteless paintings. Machines smothered her presence on either side. The clock hanging over the door and the bright stars sprinkled in the night sky told her it was eight in the evening.

Her baby.

She suddenly gasped.

"Jake!" she wailed out in what should have been her voice, but a hoarse cry echoed in the room.

She felt a jolt at her side. It was only then she realized the warm grip clutching at her fingers. She looked down to see Jake's tired eyes, levelling to meet hers.

"You're awake." He leaned over and kissed her with a hungry essence that would have woken an extinct volcano.

"I am now." She laughed tiredly. "The baby?"

“We have a beautiful little boy, Jess,” he told her, joy sparkling in his eyes.

“A little boy,” she repeated quietly to herself with amazement. “I have a son.” Her sobs came then, and she tried to control the hot tears from falling, but no matter how much she wiped them away, more fell in their place. “I told you it would be a boy,” she taunted, poking him.

“He looks like you. A lot like you.”

The only thing she recognized in his smile was adoration.

“And another thing.”

She watched his sharp jawline tense before swallowing hard. For a long moment, he did nothing. He sat there, staring straight at her. His gaze was so intense she could feel her body heat and her heart pound.

“Looks like you are coming home with me after all.”

“Of course I am,” she answered, furrowing her brows in confusion. Where did he expect her to go?

“Jess, I’m talking about the operation. They took away the cancer. It spread a little, but they said they can treat it. You’re going to be fine.”

And for the first time, Jessica saw Jake’s eyes brim with tears. She could always tell when he had been crying. His eyes looked sore and blotchy. But not once had she witnessed the man shed a tear. Not even at his mother’s funeral.

Slowly, and ever so gently, she caressed his skin with her fingertips, teasing away the tears that were threatening to spill. Before she could move her hand, he pressed his warm cheek against her palm, followed by a sweet kiss.

The kiss was so simple, yet so exhilarating.

“I told you I was going to be fine,” she whispered, smiling as he roamed over her face. He looked—she didn’t even know—helpless. Lost. She didn’t know what it was, but she wanted to hold him.

“Jessica.” Her doctor came striding into the room, totally unaware of the blissful moment he interrupted. “How is our new mommy?”

“I’m doing good.”

“I’m guessing the new father has given you the good news,” he said while giving her a quick once over.

He was about to sit down on the edge of the bed, and she guessed he was going to tell her about the treatment and blah blah blah. She didn’t want to know right now.

“Can I see my son?” she questioned, placing her loose curls behind her ears.

"Just give yourself another few minutes to gather your surroundings. You are going to be in a little pain, but I'll have a nurse come in here to get you with a wheelchair and bring you downstairs to see him." Doctor Harris grinned from ear to ear, turning on his heels and striding out of the room to do as he said.

Ten minutes later, she was sitting next to her baby, holding his hand for the first time.

"He's perfect." There was no other way to explain the little face sleeping next to her. "He's so tiny," she whispered in fear she would startle him if she spoke any louder.

"I know." Jake pulled over a chair to sit beside her. "Congratulations, Mommy." He placed his hand on the back of her chair and tangled his fingers around the loose curls that were falling onto her back.

"You too, Daddy."

She sat back and leaned into him.

"Have you thought of a name?"

She forgot about that. But she didn't have to look at him again to know it. It should have been the most obvious.

"Jay." She shrugged, enjoying the warm feeling it brought to her. "Both of our names start with that letter. It's simple but beautiful."

"You just created a tradition." Jake kissed her temple before pulling her back into his arms. "Nice thinking, Connors."

"We have our own little family thing going on now."

"Yeah, we do," he agreed, but he sounded like he was somewhere else. "You know what would make this even more perfect than what it is?"

"What?" she breathed, glancing up at him and back to Jay, lying there without a care in the world. She was sure nothing else could make this time any more beautiful.

He stayed silent for a moment, shuffling his hands through his hair.

"If you would marry me?"

She was looking at him as if he was totally mad now—her mouth hanging open, her eyes wide, and her wild hair falling onto her face. Or maybe she was the one who looked mad.

He reached into his pocket, pulling out a small, black, velvet-covered box, and opened it.

She gasped inwardly, feeling her lungs expand as a band of circular diamonds glinted under the light.

"Jake that's your—"

"My mother's ring," he cut her off. "My father gave it to me when I went to tell him you were pregnant."

She noticed how his leg was bouncing nervously.

"So, are you just going to sit there all night and look at me, or are you going to answer me and make this the best September 15th ever? Jessica Connors, will you marry me?"

Now her heart was going to explode and shatter her into a thousand pieces. She loved him so much, and without him in her life—it wasn't even worth bearing the thought.

So, it was no surprise when the word that flowed from her mouth next was the easiest she ever said.

"Yes."

THIRTY-ONE

"Come on, Jess. Get your ass moving. You're already late." April huffed around Jessica's old bedroom at her parents' house. The place was a mess. Her bed was full of makeup, hairspray, perfumes, and other feminine toiletries.

"The bride has to be fashionably late. And just because you're the maid of honour, doesn't mean you can boss me around."

April rolled her eyes and went about fixing Jessica's long veil.

"Who has Jay?"

"Mom," April answered quickly, blowing the strands of her blonde hair from her makeup-perfected face.

Sharon strolled in, so laid back she could be in a coma, swinging her arms from side to side in an identical dress to April's. She just threw herself on the bed with the same elegance as a piece of lard.

"I swear if you wrinkle that dress," Jessica warned her.

"Don't get your knickers in a twist. That's what got you into this mess in the first place," Sharon retorted. "You look beautiful." She pointed towards her lazily.

"Thank you."

"You nervous?"

"Strangely enough, no. It's only going to be Jake at the end of the aisle."

"God, you two make me sick," Sharon gagged mockingly.

"The car is here, love," her father shouted from downstairs.

Maybe she was a little nervous. Everything was happening so fast. Just six months ago, she was in the hospital, not sure if she was ever going to leave it.

But this was it.

Jake was the one.

And she didn't need time to think about it, especially after what they both went through.

"I'll follow you both down," she told them before they left the room.

Jessica turned to look at herself in the full-length mirror. Her white lace dress was straight, with a long train travelling behind from her waistline. The strapless corset fell in a V shape and continued into the simple flowing bottom, which hugged her every curve and accented her figure. Her long curls flowed down her back. A diamond hairpiece placed gracefully in her hair secured the lace floor-length veil.

Biting on her red-painted lip, she hoped the makeup artist would have an amazing life because she made the bruise-like circles engraved under Jessica's eyes disappear.

It was the treatment.

It was making her tired.

So, before she became any weaker than what she felt, she lifted her dress and headed for the stairs to marry the man she couldn't live without.

***

The clinking of a wine glass knocked her out of her trance. Her eyes roamed around the large hall. Guests were seated, enjoying a beautiful meal.

The day was perfect. The church was beautifully lit, flowers lining the pews on either side as she elegantly—well, as elegantly as she knew how—walked up the aisle to the Wedding March. Jake's smile was so big and infectious, it made her heart swell with overwhelming adoration for him. And that was all that mattered. Just seeing him there, happy and proud. It may have been a bumpy road to get them there, but they did it. And he stood by her, holding her hand through the journey.

Jay was quite content, sleeping through the whole ceremony, but having her little man there meant so much.

Her miracle.

That was the only way she knew how to describe him. He was her little miracle.

They held the reception in an old castle with the most amazing gardens Jessica had ever seen.

She turned to say something to Jake, but she was met with the material of his black tuxedo.

"Jake, what are you doing?" She tugged at his crisp white shirt.

"I'm making a speech," he said casually, staring down at her.

"You could hardly say your vows. What are you doing making a speech?" she demanded under her breath.

"Hush, Jess. Just sit back and listen to me ramble on about how amazing you are. It's sickening, really, and I have a feeling Sharon is going to throw up the contents of the dinner we just paid for."

She was nervous. What was he going to say?

"I would like to thank everyone for coming," he started, and she felt her stomach tie in a thousand knots as he spoke. "It has been the most amazing day, but I think everyone can agree that Jess, my new wife, has made the most beautiful bride."

She blushed a bright pink as everyone cheered. The heckles mostly came from three tables at the back where Jake's friends sat.

"Calm down, guys. I got her first," he hollered at them. "But I'm standing here today to tell you all just how lucky I am. For those of you who have known either of us for a long time, you will know we were never exactly best friends," he trailed off.

More laughter.

"But it didn't take long for me to realize that I loved her all along. Of course, she was too stubborn to admit anything apart from she hated me."

Another round of laughter.

"But her strength is undeniable. Falling in love with Jess was the best thing that ever happened to me. She has given me a son. A little boy she almost gave her life for. That alone shows exactly what kind of person she is. But with a combination of breath-taking beauty, a sense of humour that can have me laughing in seconds, and the charm that any man would fall for, she has become a wonderful mother, a best friend, and someone that I promise to love for the rest of my life. Now a toast to my beautiful wife. To Jess."

Everyone stood and cheered as he leaned over and covered her mouth with his. Nuzzling his face in her neck, she quickly wiped the tears away from her eyes.

"That was beautiful. Thank you." She kissed him again. "I love you. I always will, Jake."

A while later, he was leading her onto the dance floor for their first dance. Surrounded by all the people she so deeply loved, it was overwhelming to be standing there, swaying to the sweet music filling her ears. This was exactly where she belonged, in his arms for him to hold her tight, her cheek pressed against his neck.

"You know, I had it all planned out," she told him, her lips close to his ear.

"You had what all planned out?"

"How I was going to die."

He flinched, but didn't stop her.

"I didn't want to die in the hospital. I wanted to go home and be with you and Jay. I wanted you to wrap me in your arms and tell you how much I loved you. I wanted to kiss you so hard you would never forget it. I accepted I would only have so long with you. Not now." She let out a long breath. "Here I am, standing in my wedding dress, dancing my first dance with the man I love."

"But you are here now. You don't have to accept anything. And you can come and be in my arms any time you like. You can tell me how much you love me any time you like too. You don't have a time limit on that anymore, baby. You have no idea how good that feels. To have you here in my arms. You're not going anywhere, Jess. I love you too much to let you go. I always have."

Then he pulled her closer and gently pressed his lips to hers, remaining like that as they swayed throughout their first dance.

Later that night, Jessica strolled out of the bathroom, fumbling over her steps as Jake sneaked behind her, nudging his fingers into her flesh.

"Hey, beautiful."

"Hey."

"Your Mom took Jay home to our house. The music was too loud for him."

"Okay." She nodded, making a mental note to thank her mother for how good she was being. Maybe it was because he was the first grandchild, but she had seriously spoiled him.

"You'll never guess what?"

"What?" she giggled, rolling her eyes.

"Come outside and I will show you. You're going to love it." He waved his hands, taunting her to follow him.

"Jake, it's the middle of March. I'm not going outside," she demanded, thinking he was a crazy person. A very sexy, crazy person.

"Come on, you can have my jacket," he said, shrugging his arms out of his black coat and wrapping it around her shoulders. "Now come on." He grabbed her hands, tugging her until she caught up.

And he was right. She loved it. White crystal snowdrops were gathering on the ground, blanketing the concrete beneath them.

"Oh wow. It's snowing," she breathed in disbelief.

The sparkling stars decorated the night, shining down on them both.

"I love the stars," she whispered as he wrapped his arms around her waist and tugged her closer. He trailed loving kisses down the soft skin of her neck and onto her shoulder.

"You know if anything ever happens to me?"

"Jess," Jake begged.

"No. I'm serious. Not just this cancer. If anything were to happen. Tell Jay I'm a star in the sky, always watching over him. Promise?"

"I promise, but you're not going anywhere."

"Just in case," she murmured.

"Just in case," he agreed.

"Jake?"

"Uh-huh?"

"I know we have a room here at the hotel, but let's go home tonight."

"If that's what you want. I'd prefer to go home too. I'm missing my little man, and I can tell you're not feeling well."

"I'm fine," she pressed, leaning her head back on his shoulder. The snow was still falling on them both, but neither cared.

She turned to face him, feeling her chest rise and fall frantically.

"Take me home now, Jake," she almost begged, tears glistening in her eyes.

"Okay, sweetheart," he agreed, concerned with the look in her eyes. She looked sick. He could see it, but it didn't differ from how she had been looking since she started the treatment. The makeup was fading now. The dark circles around her eyes were more prominent, and her lips were pale.

So, he did as she asked, and he took her home to where she

belonged.

"What are you two doing back here?" Rose woke from sleeping on the sofa.

"You can go home, Mom. Dad must miss you." Jessica kissed her mother's cheek.

"It would be nice to have my own bed, honey. But I hope you didn't come back because of me. Jay has been a little angel."

"No, I wanted my bed too."

Jessica gathered her mother's coat and helped her as she slipped her arms through the sleeves.

"I love you," she told her before they both waved her off from the door and watched her drive away.

Grabbing her dress in her hands so she wouldn't trip, Jessica slowly made her way upstairs with Jake following close behind.

"Will you unzip this at the back?"

"Sure," he said, stepping behind her, crawling the delicate zip down her back, uncovering the pale bare skin. He kissed the nape of her neck again and let his fingers crawl down her arms. She gasped quietly, indulging in his scent, his movement, his feel, but surprisingly, even to herself, she pulled away.

"Before any of that." She smiled evilly. "I'm going to check on Jay. Get changed," she ordered before she stepped into a black satin nightdress.

Damn that woman! She drove him crazy.

Instead of changing, he quickly threw cold water on his face and followed her into the nursery, but she was already fast asleep with Jay snoring quietly over her shoulder.

Carefully, Jake picked him up, kissed his soft cheek, and placed him back in his crib before doing the same with Jess. She looked exhausted as he laid her delicately on the bed. The day, along with the severe treatments, had taken a toll on her. He covered her and kissed her gently, but just as he went to walk away, she grabbed his hand. Her eyes were still closed.

"I don't care if you are fully dressed, naked, or in a banana suit. Just get your ass into bed with me." Her laugh was hoarse and weak.

"Of course," he obliged, throwing off his shoes and cuddling up next to her so that she was lying comfortably in his arms.

She tilted her head to lock her eyes with his, and then she kissed him. Kissing him like he'd never been kissed before. Every feeling she ever had poured out of her soul and into him with one touch of her body against his.

He groaned as she did the impossible—she deepened the kiss, exploring every inch of him until he was left totally defenceless and both of their breathing was frantic.

She pulled away and leaned her head on his chest.

"I love you so much. Always," was the last thing she said before she dozed off into the darkness of her sleep.

THIRTY-TWO

Jake woke to the bright beam of light escaping through his window. The smell of Jessica's auburn hair, which was enriched with some sort of vanilla scent, awakened his senses.

"Rise and shine, Mrs. Williams." He nudged her and smothered his lips in her curls.

Wow, it felt good to say that.

Memories of her elegance and how she took her steps towards him in the church the day before. She was simply breath-taking. He promised himself he wouldn't cry, but seeing her and remembering all she fought so hard for, the tears streamed with no consideration of his promises.

To him, every day she was beautiful, but frankly, he'd never seen anything so perfect as Jess as a bride. She had stolen his breath, his heart, and even his mind.

She was his.

Forever.

"Sweetheart, wake up." He hugged her closer.

She really was a nightmare in the mornings.

Staying still as he could, he smoothed his hand over the silk of her nightdress.

Still no movement.

Not even for her breath.

But when he didn't feel her exhale on his skin, he shook her.

"Jess, wake up," he panicked.

He turned her on her back so that he was hovering over her lifeless body, desperate to see a flicker in her eyes.

"Jess, baby, you have to wake up."

He touched her pale skin. She was still warm when he caressed her cheeks with his fingertips.

"Jess?"

She couldn't leave him.

Not now.

But she wasn't moving. She wasn't breathing either, and her body hung limp. He leaned his forehead against hers, not feeling any breath on his face.

She should be opening her eyes.

"Beautiful?" he whispered.

But something tugging at his heart told him this was a sleep he wouldn't be able to wake her from.

EPILOGUE

6 years later…

Jake sat in his car outside of the old school building, remembering everything about the short time he had with his beautiful wife.

She knew in her heart that night was going to be her last with him.

Her words replayed in his head. "I wanted to go home and be with you and Jay. I wanted you to wrap me in your arms and tell you how much I loved you. I wanted to kiss you so hard you would never forget it."

She was telling him—trying to get through to him—she knew in her soul it was going to be her last night. She didn't want to die in a hotel suite. She wanted to be at home with him and her son, just like she said.

She may not have been with him anymore, but he could still feel her, and every now and again, her scent would fill his senses, and he knew she was there.

Jessica Connors was someone he would never let go, never forget, and always love.

The sound of screaming children running out of the school building like a herd of elephants interrupted his thoughts. He quickly stepped out of the car, crossed the road to the other side of the street, and sat on the wall, waiting for what was now his life to appear.

With a small backpack bobbling on his back, his coat was swinging from his arms and his dark auburn hair was rustled and messy as he played with another little boy. The minute he spotted Jake, he ran to him.

"Hey, kiddo." Jake messed his hair even more by running his fingers through it.

"Hey, Dad." He looked up at him with bright blue eyes.

Jake swore he was getting more like her every single day.

"Why is your coat not on you? I bought it to keep you warm, not for you to hold it."

"I was too hot," Jay complained, grunting.

"Come on, buddy, put it on." Jake ignored the loud sigh and the clicking of his son's tongue against the roof of his mouth.

"You've forgotten something," Jay reminded him, smiling at him with a mischievous grin.

"No, I haven't. I only came to get my son." Jake stopped, glancing behind him, playing dumb.

"You forgot to say something to me. It's one of those days when you have to get a super present."

"Well." Jake thought. "It's not Christmas yet. I wonder why I would have to buy you a super present."

"It's my birthday, Dad. I'm six today."

"It is?" He rolled his eyes. "Well, of course it is."

Jake leaned over to tickle him before swooping him up onto his shoulders.

"I think you've forgotten. I already wished you a happy birthday this morning."

"Yeah, I know," Jay droned, giggling as he wrapped his arms around Jake's neck.

"So, you're six today. Let me feel those muscles." Jake held a tight grip on his son's upper arm. "Whoa, before you know it, you'll be carrying me on your shoulders."

"What? No way, Dad. You're too big."

Carefully, Jake lowered him from his shoulders and strapped him into the back seat of the car.

"Where are we going?" he asked as Jake drove off.

"You'll see."

Kids, Jake thought, *they're always so full of questions.*

"Grandma and Grandpa's house." Jay looked mystified as they

pulled up outside the blue-painted house. Jake could imagine the chaos from inside, everyone trying to gather around in one large huddle.

"Happy Birthday," they shouted out in unison as they stepped inside. The entire family, including his father, was standing in the living room with some of Jay's friends.

"This is so cool." Jay swallowed, but his cheeks flushed a pale red.

Something his mother would have done if she were in the same position.

"Happy birthday, sweetie." Rose leaned down to kiss her grandson on the cheek.

"Thanks, Grandma." He smiled, his musical voice resonating around the room.

Every other person in the room followed with more kisses and hugs, smothering him with affection and love.

"Thanks, Dad," he said as Jake lowered down to his knees to kiss his son—the son that resembled Jess so much it hurt. But it hurt in a good way. It reminded him of how amazing and how selfless she was to leave behind such a beautiful little boy. "I love you, Dad."

Jake swallowed the bitter-sweet lump growing in his throat.

"No problem, kiddo. I love you too. Now go play with your friends for a bit. You can open your presents later."

Jay didn't need to be told twice. He was gone like the wind.

Then the screams came. The endless screams of eight children. Wasn't that just fantastic?

"Hey, Jake." April kissed his cheek.

"Where is this new boyfriend of yours, so I can rough him up a little?"

"Shut up, Jake. Besides, he's a cop." Jake didn't care what he was. "He couldn't make it today," she explained.

"Lucky guy."

"I agree. No guy messes with my little sister." Pete threw an arm around April's shoulders. "We'd have to slap him around a bit. It's a welcoming gift."

"What are you talking about, Pete? You married Sharon and got her knocked up," Jake teased his brother-in-law, nodding his head in fake disbelief.

Sharon growled as she plopped herself on the sofa, positioning her denim dungarees around her large bump.

"Shut up. Don't be an asshole."

"Are you still pregnant? You can't keep it in there forever."

"Please don't remind me, Jake. I'm already in enough pain as it is," she begged breathlessly.

Jake sat beside her and patted her thigh.

"When are you due?"

"Last week," she answered, frustration boiling in her voice.

Poor Pete, he thought. He couldn't deal with Sharon on a good day. A pregnant day must have been hell.

But he could see she wanted her best friend with her to hold her hand and laugh at her when she was getting out of control.

"You'll be fine. Don't forget to call when it finally arrives."

"I won't."

Later that evening, when the children had left, everyone gathered around the table in the dining room, reminiscing and remembering those who should have been there. It was only then Jake noticed the rest of the house was painfully quiet.

He excused himself, leaving to find his son.

The darkness was creeping in around them, and the small lamp was the only light illuminating the hallway. That's where he found him, standing there, staring up at a large picture frame on the wall.

His heart sank.

It was a photo of his and Jess's wedding.

"What are you doing?"

"Looking at Mom."

Jake lifted him into his arms so that he could get a better view.

"Wasn't she beautiful?"

"Yeah." Jay nodded, a somber look in his blue eyes. "Why isn't she here anymore?"

Jay had asked this question a million times before.

"She got sick. God needed a new helper, so she had to leave."

"But everyone else has a mom, and I don't."

Jake swallowed hard, wiping away the tears that were threatening to fall.

Poor kid, he thought, none of this was fair to him.

Jake knew what it was like to lose his mother, but at least he had the chance to get to know her first.

"I need to bring you out to the backyard, okay?"

"Why?".

"Because I need to show you something."

Jake set him on his feet when they were outside and sat on the cold step beneath them.

"Your mother loved you very much," Jake explained. "And she was so proud of you. She still is."

"What do you mean? Still?"

"Even though she had to leave, she's still here with us."

"Where?" Jay furrowed his eyebrows, wrinkling his nose in confusion.

"Look up at the sky and tell me what you see."

"I see the stars," he answered, straining his tiny neck.

"Your Mom is up there."

"Mom is a star?" His mouth fell open.

"Uh-huh." Jake nodded. "But not just any star. I want you to find the brightest star."

Jay spun around a few times, searching the darkness of the night sky, until he came to a sudden halt and pointed straight above him.

"There!"

"That's her. She's the brightest star up there."

"Whoa. That's cool." His eyes widened as he sat again, not once taking his eyes from the star above him.

"Any time you think of her, or any time you want to talk to her—you might just want to know she's there—look out the window or go outside and look for the brightest star you can find, because that is where she is, and she's always going to be looking down on you." Jake stroked his hand over his son's back.

"I can call her Twinkle Star like the song," Jay suggested proudly.

"That's a great idea." Jake laughed.

"I love you, Mom," Jay announced, loud enough for the entire house to hear.

Jake stared up at the sky then and found the brightest star he could. "I love you, Jess," he breathed.

But he didn't need the sparkle of a star to tell him just how much.

"On the count of three, we are going to blow her a kiss, okay?"

"Okay," Jay agreed, his hand already over his mouth.

"One. Two. Three."

And they both blew her the most loving kiss they could muster.

Jake chuckled under his breath because something inside was telling him she was up there smiling, catching their kisses, and keeping them very close to her heart.

We love hearing your thoughts.
If you enjoyed Watch Over My Life, please consider leaving a review on Amazon or Goodreads.

What Will Be Book Series

There are many organizations offering information and support around the issues involved in the book. The following do invaluable work:

The Irish Cancer Society www.cancer.ie

Marie Keating Foundation www.mariekeating.ie

Safe Ireland www.safeireland.ie

Ingram Content Group UK Ltd.
Milton Keynes UK
UKHW040207110423
419909UK00018BA/669